WYNDHAM

THE CHRYSALIDS, THE DAY OF THE TRIFFIDS

NOTES

ALTA VISTA

COLES EDITORIAL BOARD

Bound to stay open

Publisher's Note

Otabind (Ota-bind). This book has been bound using the patented Otabind process. You can open this book at any page, gently run your finger down the spine, and the pages will lie flat.

ABOUT COLES NOTES

COLES NOTES have been an indispensible aid to students on five continents since 1948.

COLES NOTES are available for a wide range of individual literary works. Clear, concise explanations and insights are provided along with interesting interpretations and evaluations.

Proper use of COLES NOTES will allow the student to pay greater attention to lectures and spend less time taking notes. This will result in a broader understanding of the work being studied and will free the student for increased participation in discussions.

COLES NOTES are an invaluable aid for review and exam preparation as well as an invitation to explore different interpretive paths.

COLES NOTES are written by experts in their fields. It should be noted that any literary judgement expressed herein is just that – the judgement of one school of thought. Interpretations that diverge from, or totally disagree with any criticism may be equally valid.

COLES NOTES are designed to supplement the text and are not intended as a substitute for reading the text itself. Use of the NOTES will serve not only to clarify the work being studied, but should enhance the readers enjoyment of the topic.

ISBN 0-7740-3722-9

© COPYRIGHT 1998 AND PUBLISHED BY
COLES PUBLISHING COMPANY
TORONTO - CANADA
PRINTED IN CANADA

Manufactured by Webcom Limited
Cover finish: Webcom's Exclusive **DURACOAT**

CONTENTS

THE DAY OF THE TRIFFIDS

John Wyndham: Life and Works

John Wyndham was born in England, on July 10, 1903 and was christened John Wyndham Parkes Lucas Beynon Harris. He wrote English science fiction stories under the names "John Beynon Harris," "John Beynon" and "Lucas Parkes," as well as John Wyndham.

When Wyndham was growing up, he went to a series of boarding schools because his parents were separated. He then attended an advanced co-educational school until he reached the age of eighteen. After he left school, Wyndham studied farming for awhile, then "crammed" to write the examinations for Oxford University. He then changed his mind again and tried advertising. He wrote a great many short stories, as well, but without much success.

Finally, in 1929, Wyndham picked up a copy of an American magazine called *Amazing Stories*, and became very interested in science fiction. Not long after that a series of science fiction short stories under the name of John Beynon began to appear in *Amazing Stories*, and in another publication called *Wonder Stories*.

By 1935, John Beynon had published his first novel, *The Secret People*, which was serialized in Canada in *The Star Weekly*. By 1937, he was being called the best, living British science fiction writer.

Wyndham worked for the British government from 1940 to 1943, but went into the army in time to participate in the Normandy invasion. He was a corporal cipher operator in the Royal Signal Corps. After the war he began writing again and, this time, he used the name John Wyndham.

The Day of the Triffids (1951) was his first major science fiction work. Its success led quickly to the publication of others. *The Kraken Wakes* appeared in 1953 and *The Chrysalids* was published in 1955. *The Midwich Cuckoos* (1957) was Wyndham's last important science fiction novel, before he died in 1969.

Wyndham's work in science fiction is interesting in its emphasis. He does not generally concentrate on amusing the reader with strange inventions of technology from a bewildering future. The settings he employs for the future are logical, identifiable extensions of the world of today. For example,

1

though the people of *The Chrysalids* inhabit a village with the strange name of Waknuk, the world they are coping with is essentially our world after it has been devastated by a hydrogen bomb. Similarly, in *The Day of the Triffids*, the setting of Bill Masen's world is not unfamiliar. It is England as it might be in a few years, not a strange land with strange customs and strange technology. Of course, Bill Masen's world is facing a crisis unfamiliar to us. It has been visited by blinding radiation and it is ravaged by deadly triffids. Nevertheless, many features of the life of his world are familiar. This aspect of Wyndham's work does, perhaps, give a clue to his major interest in science fiction. His consuming interest lay in speculation about human nature and human behavior. This would account for his attention to customs and moral codes displayed in the different societies in his books. Thus, time and again he seems to point out the hypocrisy, bigotry and ignorance which are so often a part of our social life, and time and again he seems to stress that changing conditions demand new ways, new customs and new codes of conduct. Thus, though Wyndham could undoubtedly write stories that feature exciting episodes and thrilling situations, social considerations were at the heart of his work.

The Day of the Triffids and *The Midwich Cuckoos* were made into successful films. The movie screen has, if anything, increased the reputation of John Wyndham, for the motion picture presentations of his stories underline what is, perhaps, their most effective point. As science fiction, they are terrifyingly believable.

Science Fiction—A Brief History

In the 1920s, unsold science fiction magazines were used as ballast in ships travelling from the United States to England. Such an ignominious use shows how comparatively recent is the respectability of popular science fiction.

Not that it is a new form. A Greek prose romancer of the classical period, Lucian of Samosata, wrote a volume entitled *True History*. It dealt with interplanetary travel, but purposely indulged in comic extravaganza and mocked itself.

In 1634, Kepler, an Englishman, described a moon voyage on a raft pulled by demons. Five years later, Bishop Godwin wrote *Man in the Moone, or A Discourse of a Voyage Thither by Domingo Gonsales*. In each case, however, the stories had a moral purpose.

Others followed these men, but not until the nineteenth century did the science fiction form gain vital popularity with the writings of Jules Verne. Both Verne and the next great science fiction writer, H. G. Wells, wrote items that were known as romances or adventures. These works were still regarded as amusing oddities and did not enjoy distinction as a separate genre.

After 1940, the form began to gain respect as a separate entity but, then, the form, too, began to change. Technological advances during World War II left the monster stories and much of the space travel to pulp writers. Most good science fiction today involves some form of social comment. Strangely enough, what began as a form dealing strictly with alien forces is now at its best when dealing with what we might do to ourselves.

THE CHRYSALIDS

Introduction

Science fiction demands a certain suspension of disbelief on the part of the reader. For example, light-year speed is explained away by the term "space warp" or "warp speed," and the reader accepts this. (Western stories don't explain how to run a ranch either!) But, generally, science fiction has a healthy respect for fact.

The Chrysalids maintains this respect. It is not at all "way-out" science fiction. There are only two assumptions: that a nuclear holocaust took place to destroy civilization as we know it, and that certain members of Waknuk can communicate through mental telepathy.

Both of these factors are based on truth or, at least, scientifically accepted possibility. The threat of Tribulation, although we don't call it that, needs no explanation for a twentieth-century reader. As far as the group's ability is concerned, many major universities now have departments of parapsychology in which mental telepathy, psychometry, dream communication and so on, are studied under scientifically controlled conditions.

As a form of science fiction, *The Chrysalids* is remarkable, for it presents a tantalizingly possible, yet improbable, situation with a fascinating degree of credibility. Once Wyndham makes the two fictional assumptions, he never moves beyond the limits established. The society of Waknuk is perfectly plausible, as are the characters in it. Deviations, we know, are a real result of radiation. Even the telepathic abilities of the group are not the same in each member. The only flaw might be the Sealand people, but even this group falls within the limits established.

One more thing the genre usually accomplishes is to suggest infinite possibilities for the future, *outside* the novel. Whereas more conventional stories often finish with happy-ever-after endings, and all complications are neatly unravelled, science fiction stories often leave a number of unanswered possibilities. This is probably the justification of the Sealand people in the story. The Sealand lady glows with excitement when she reflects on the unknown possibilities open to people who can think together. Another unanswered possibility is left to the reader: what are the likely effects of a nuclear war?

The word "chrysalid" is a scientific term meaning the state into which the larvae of most insects pass before becoming adults. In general usage, the word can mean a sheltered state or a stage of growth. Thus, as with all good titles, the reader of *The Chrysalids* is left to extend this definition so as to apply it in an appropriate way to the novel itself.

Plot Summary

In *The Chrysalids*, John Wyndham relates the story of a small group of people who are living in the part of the world we know as Labrador.

The society of Waknuk has survived a nuclear war (Tribulation, as it is known in the book), but radiation has contaminated the living things outside the small community. Whenever any evidence of contamination is found within Waknuk, the inhabitants immediately eliminate the offending person, plant or animal.

The story centers around the narrator, David Strorm, his friends, all of whom possess E.S.P. or extrasensory perception, and David's sternly religious family.

As a child, David quickly learned the strict morality of his society. This morality meant that any living thing—plant, animal or man—had to be destroyed as soon as it was discovered to be deviant. David's father, Joseph Strorm, was considered by the inhabitants of the community of Waknuk to be a model in the vigorous pursuit of deviations from the norm.

Waknuk, though, was relatively fortunate. Since God had sent Tribulation down upon the Old People, mankind had been struggling to return to the level of civilization that the Old People had enjoyed. Because the past generations of Waknuk had been very careful, the community was now fairly free of deviations that were the result of Tribulation. Any that did appear were destroyed or, in the case of deviant humans, banished to the Fringes country that surrounded the district.

At the beginning of the story David meets Sophie Wender and discovers that she is a physical deviant with six toes. Both she and her family are forced to flee to the Fringes. David finds it difficult to reconcile the laws of his society with his own conscience. This problem is intensified when he sees his aunt driven to suicide.

David is concerned for his own personal safety when he realizes that he and his friends are also deviants. They possess the ability to communicate with each other in thought forms or by mental telepathy. This power is not compatible with Waknuk's idea of the "true image."

Although they manage to disguise their deviation, the birth of David's little sister, Petra, causes innumerable problems. She has such strong telepathic powers that she is able to communicate with a strange, distant civilization. Because Petra is unable to control her powers, an incident occurs in which she, David and his sweetheart, Rosalind, are declared deviates and outlaws, and are forced to flee to the Fringes.

They are pursued by the people of Waknuk, right into the Fringes, where David, Petra and Rosalind have been captured by the strange inhabitants there.

All this time, Petra has kept in touch with a distant civilization in New Zealand (Sealand). These people, who are *all* telepathic, rescue the fugitives and take them away to their country just as the Waknuk and Fringes people engage in battle.

Characters in the Novel

The Strorm Family

DAVID STRORM: Hero of the novel; possesses a peculiar telepathic ability which causes the main conflict in the novel.

JOSEPH STRORM: David's father; champion of purity in all forms of life; leading figure in Waknuk.

EMILY STRORM: David's mother.

PETRA STRORM: David's younger sister; possesses awesome telepathic powers; causes crisis of the novel and ultimately brings rescue.

AUNT HARRIET: Emily's sister; gives birth to a deviate and, after failing to conceal it, commits suicide.

MARY STRORM: David's older sister; somewhat sympathetic to him.

UNCLE AXEL: David's uncle; knows about David's ability; broad-minded and philosophical; acts as protector of David during the latter's youth.

ELIAS STRORM: David's grandfather; not part of the novel but was founder of the community of Waknuk, and largely responsible for its philosophy.

SPIDER MAN: The older brother of Joseph ·Strorm; deprived of his rights as a boy because of deviational arms and legs; lives in the Fringes.

The Group

DAVID

PETRA

MICHAEL: Eldest of the group; best educated; acts as leader and philosopher.

ROSALIND MORTON: David's half-cousin and sweetheart; flees with him to the Fringes.

ANNE: Only member of the group to violate its solidarity; marries a norm; dies violently.

RACHEL: Anne's sister; loyal to the group.

KATHERINE: First to be discovered by Waknuk; under torture, reveals David, Rosalind and Petra.

SALLY: Neighbor of Katherine; captured with her.

MARK: Lives farthest from the group; along with Michael and Rachel, he is not discovered.

The Others

SOPHIE WENDER: Childhood friend of David; discovered as a deviate and banished to the Fringes; most pathetic victim of Waknuk's fury.

THE WENDERS: Martie and Johnny, Sophie's parents; because they concealed Sophie, they, too, were banished.

ANGUS MORTON: Rosalind's father; in constant feud with Joseph Strorm over deviations; seems to be more intelligent than his enemy.

OLD JACOB: Keeper at Strorm farm; ultra-right-wing believer in Waknuk religion.

ALAN ERVIN: Anne's husband; had reported Sophie Wender; dies a violent death.

THE SEALAND LADY: Woman in distant civilization who communicates with Petra.

JEROME SKINNER: Stranger to Waknuk, but partially responsible for discovery of some of the group.

THE INSPECTOR: Responsible for purity in Waknuk; carries authority of the government in Rigo; a reasonable man, but not intelligent enough to think his way past the limits of his job.

Chapter by Chapter Summaries
and Commentaries

CHAPTER 1

A Dream and the Definition

Summary

As a very young child, David Strorm often had a curious dream, a dream of a city on a big, blue bay, with boats in the harbor, and strange carts on the streets with no horses pulling them. When he awoke, the dream always became doubly strange, for he had never even seen the sea, much less a boat and, certainly, he had never seen such buildings before. When he recounted the dream to his elder sister, Mary, she suggested that perhaps he was dreaming of times long ago, when the Old People lived in their wonderful world—before God had sent Tribulation. But Mary also cautioned him not to tell anyone about the dream, for people in their district did not take very kindly to the odd or the unusual. Consequently, David told no one of his dream, nor did he tell anyone about the curious understanding he had with his cousin, Rosalind: they could exchange thought patterns.

It wasn't until the day he met Sophie that David began to think about differences in people. He had been sliding down the sand bank in one of his favorite secluded spots when she first peeked through the bushes. Her small, sunburned face was surrounded by dark curls. Sophie loved excitement, and it didn't take long to persuade her to try the sand bank. It wasn't until the third try that the accident happened. Her left foot sank into the soft sand and was caught between two stones. At first, Sophie fought against having her shoe removed but, eventually, she had to give in. David was so concerned about Sophie's hurt foot, though, that he didn't even notice her six toes.

Sophie impressed David with her stamina and determination to get home unassisted, but he finally had to run to Sophie's house to get her mother. The house was in a part of the country that was strange to David but he found it quickly.

In the little cottage, Mrs. Wender bound the foot carefully, with a look of real anxiety on her face. Later, she clasped David with both hands and, with a frightened earnestness, made him promise never to reveal to anyone the strangeness of Sophie's feet. David could read the fear in her thoughts but, when he tried to return a statement of reassurance in thought patterns, he knew she didn't understand, so he tried to express his sincerity in words.

Only on the way home did the impact of Sophie's six toes reach him. Sophie was a mutant! Her feet made her a clear violation of the Definition of Man, which specifically stated that "each foot shall have five toes." Anything not formed according to the Definition was not human, and was a blasphemy against God. But Sophie didn't seem at all hateful. As a matter of fact, she seemed quite ordinary. At the age of ten, David found his world a rather strange place.

Commentary

The strongest impact made in the first chapter is not so much that of the main character, David, as the number of questions raised by his narration. Sophie's six toes are unusual, but why should Mrs. Wender be so terrified that David has seen them? Her fear suggests more than just the worry of a social stigma. Why do the Wenders live so far from the rest of the people in the area? Why did Mary warn David against telling others of his dream? What is David's curious understanding with Rosalind? If Mrs. Wender wears the "conventional" cross from hem to hem and from breast to breast, why is it "conventional"? Where did David get the "Definition of Man"?

Some of the questions are at least partially answered. Obviously, this is a civilization different from the one we, the readers, know. The Old People may be from our civilization or one like it, and Tribulation may be anything from a plague to a nuclear holocaust. However, Sophie's six toes and the society's obvious concern over normality seem to suggest the effects of radiation. Furthermore, the bank that David follows in his wanderings is every bit like an abandoned railroad. Thus, the Old People may quite certainly be us! And Tribulation?

Clearly, David's society is obsessed with normality. David's ability to recall religious statements on the subject by memory, at the age of ten, attests to this. The dress of the women (since Sophie, too, wore a cross) further underlines this atmosphere of strong, fundamental religion.

David, himself, seems to be a normal ten-year-old—

curious, friendly, open and frequently dismayed by the strange ways of adults. But he, too, has a characteristic far stranger than Sophie's toes. He can read people's minds, or at least sense what they are feeling. His home life is partially explained by his reflection that the Wender home, though much smaller than his own, is much friendlier. His apparent independence and ability to make a decision are qualities that will be of advantage to him.

Glossary

Sunday precepts: rules to guide or direct human behavior

Definition of Man: the religious definition of a normally formed human being as David's society believed it should be

blasphemy: by the terms of David's society, a malformed human being

offence: a malformed animal or vegetable

germinate: to begin to develop

cleft: a crack

rote: a set, mechanical way of doing things

cold-poulticed: a soft, moist mixture of mustard and herbs, spread on a cloth, and applied to a sore or injury

CHAPTER 2
Watch Thou for the Mutant

Summary

David made his way home with the usual caution exercised by the people of the area for, occasionally, wild creatures penetrated even as far as the civilized area of Waknuk. He reached the house, however, without incident, and went to his room until supper was ready.

The house was a solid one, built by David's grandfather, Elias, and added to by David's father, Joseph. Elias had come from the East, "to escape the Godless ways there." At that time Waknuk was only a frontier with just a few remnants of the Old People's buildings still there.

Although Elias's wife died very young, their son, Joseph, was strong and healthy, and survived his father to continue the evangelism the elder Strorm had established. Joseph was now the wealthiest and most influential man in the district, and both the district and his family felt the weight of his religious bent. His house was filled with panels on which were scorched sayings from *Repentances* such as *Watch thou for the mutant* and *The Devil is the father of deviation*.

It was the subject of deviation that possessed Waknuk most thoroughly, and Joseph Strorm was the district's leading example of purity. Frequently, an animal would be born on the farm with an extra, or a missing, limb. Occasionally, crops would grow unlike the parent plants. These Offences, as they were called, had to be destroyed. The entire Strorm family would gather in prayer as the deviate was slaughtered or burnt to keep pure the stock of the Lord.

Blasphemies were even worse than Offences because these were deviations in humans. Some stability had been achieved in Waknuk, however. It was only in the Wild Country that surrounded the district that the chance of breeding true was less than fifty per cent. Beyond this area was the Fringes, full of deviations, especially Blasphemies who had escaped, or who had been sterilized and sent to live out their unfortunate lives there. Frequently, the occupants of the Fringes would raid near Waknuk because there was so little for them where they lived.

There was plenty of food in David Strorm's home though. It was needed, too, for many of his relatives lived with them;

that is, except for his half-uncle Angus Morton, Rosalind's father. Unfortunately, he owned the farm next to Joseph Strorm, and the two men fought over every issue.

Few of these problems bothered David. He was more concerned with avoiding extra jobs on the farm.

Commentary

The basic purpose of this chapter is to supply answers to some of the questions raised in Chapter 1, and to fill in background information about David's family and the district of Waknuk.

The area is quite obviously settled, as is pointed out by references to the government in Rigo, and by the fact that David frequently makes reference to the advantage of being civilized. However, the Fringes and Wild Country show that civilization is not total as yet; nor is Waknuk, itself, totally free from danger.

Further evidence of the Old People's efforts again suggests that they are *us*, and that Tribulation is an event which brought about the end of our society. Thus, the story appears to be a novel of the future, even though the setting suggests a parallel with what we would know as the late seventeenth to early nineteenth century.

David's people and, certainly, his father, have an obsession with the purity of life forms. Their destruction of every deviant form of life is a bad sign for Sophie, and the fact that David's father is a leader in this struggle for purity adds suspense. Future conflict, possibly over Sophie, seems inevitable.

The introduction of the Fringes people, too, adds some suspense, for the threat of a raid is always present.

Finally, Angus Morton's presence seems to strike a different note. His opposition to Joseph Strorm's stern, unbending attitude is a welcome relief.

Glossary

Nicholson's Repentances: repentance means a turning away from the path of disobedience to the prescribed method of behavior. This book was obviously a guide to morality for the people of Waknuk.

mutant: an animal or human that has some basic physical or mental alteration; a freak

deviation: a marked departure from the accepted pattern; in David's society, mutants are deviations

midden: refuse heap or manure pile

leeward: the side away from the wind; a sheltered place

wattle: framework of twigs interlaced, used for roofs, walls and fences

wraith: a ghost

meticulousness: excessive attention to small details

CHAPTER 3

The Purification—a Dream

Summary

David's schooling was a very informal undertaking, carried out every morning by one of the older ladies. Since the afternoons were free and, since David was as adept at avoiding work as any ten-year-old, it was easy for him to spend a lot of time with Sophie. Usually, they stayed in Sophie's territory but, occasionally, they would come to David's side of the bank to watch the huge steam engine.

John Wender, however, always regarded David carefully; he never forgot that the little boy who shared the Wender secret was Joseph Strorm's son.

Sophie's father, however, would have been reassured by David's dream after the "splinter incident." About a month after David had met Sophie, he ran a splinter into his finger, and was forced to bind it himself because everyone was busy. When he commented, very casually, that the bandaging would have been a simple task if he had had a third hand, the effect was electric. Joseph Strorm went from amazement to uncontrollable fury. It was only after a long session of prayer, and a sermon on deviations and normality that David was able to crawl to bed. There, David's troubled dreams recalled the slaughter of a deviant calf that had taken place weeks before. But instead of the calf under his father's upraised knife, he saw Sophie. The terror David felt was strong insurance against his ever exposing Sophie.

Commentary

Reference to airplanes and other machinery peculiar to the twentieth century supplies further evidence toward the exact identification of the Old People.

The huge steam engine places David's society at about the level of the eighteenth or nineteenth century. It also indicates the wealth and prominence of Joseph Strorm, since there was no other such machine for a hundred miles around.

Joseph Strorm is further revealed as a man to be feared. John Wender regrets that David Strorm, of all people, shares Sophie's secret; and Joseph's reaction during the "splinter incident" demonstrates how violently he feels about deviations.

It is during the "splinter incident" that the author first begins to satirize David's society in general, and his father in particular. That the idle comments of a young boy should arouse such rage makes the Strorm religion look somewhat foolish, and Joseph himself somewhat of a fool. Certainly, he seems to be intensely narrow-minded by nature, and this unfortunate trait is nurtured by his religious beliefs.

Glossary

norm: the standard, or the average; in this case, whatever was considered normal by the teachings of the Waknuk society

implacable: that which cannot be pacified; relentless, without mercy

CHAPTER 4

The Group

Summary

A series of successive crises temporarily relieved David of his concern for Sophie. The first of these was the uncertainty of David's own society. His Uncle Axel discovered him one day behind a haystack, communicating with Rosalind by mental telepathy. Luckily for David, it was Axel who discovered him. At first, the man thought his nephew was talking to himself and teased him for it. Even when David very innocently explained what was happening, Axel didn't believe it until, finally, the boy's seriousness broke through to him. David could actually communicate using thought patterns. He was a deviate—a Blasphemy! Axel carefully warned him never to tell anyone, and urged him to warn Rosalind as well.

On the heels of this crisis came another of more general, and immediate concern—an invasion from the Fringes. By the time Waknuk was fully organized, the invaders had penetrated to within seven miles. But at this point a battle destroyed their advance and two prisoners were brought to the Strorm farm. To David's disappointment they looked almost normal, but one of them shocked him in an entirely different way. He was almost a duplicate, in appearance, of his father, Joseph! The man spoke to him and even seemed to know where he was and who owned the farm! David's shock was further emphasized when he saw his father go white at the sight of the man. The incident passed, however, and David could never bring himself to ask Joseph about it.

Hardly had this incident passed when Joseph Strorm began another argument with Angus Morton. The latter had purchased a pair of great-horses, huge animals capable of twice the work of ordinary horses for less than the cost of twice the feed. Although they were sanctioned by the government, Joseph tried to have these horses destroyed as deviations, and his failure to accomplish this only deepened the ill will toward Angus Morton.

Only when the crisis passed did David see Sophie again. Because she couldn't go to school, David, in their frequent conversations, explained the situation in Waknuk.

They were living in an area that the Old People had called Labrador, a large section of the country surrounded by the sea. It hadn't been inhabited to any great degree by the Old People because of the cold climate but, since Tribulation, only two months in the year were cold. Tribulation had changed many things. However, most of the Old People's world was unknown since only the Bible had survived. From the Age of Barbarism, which followed Tribulation, only *Nicholson's Repentances* had survived, so that anything beyond the three recorded centuries was a great blur.

The only logic David could discover in Tribulation was what he learned in Ethics on Sunday. Tribulation was another of the series of trials that came from the fall from grace, a trial like the Flood of the Old Testament. The only way out of the effects created by Tribulation, Ethics dictated, was to keep the human form free of deviations; but David didn't say much about this to Sophie.

Commentary

David first learns, although he doesn't fully understand why, that he must never reveal his strange ability to communicate using thought patterns. This extrasensory communication establishes a base for interdependence among the small group that has this ability. For the first time, they are set apart as something different.

As Axel is shown to be understanding, kind and broad-minded, so is Joseph shown to be a dangerous, self-righteous bigot, capable of operating outside the law in his fight to clear out deviations.

The strange look-alike prisoner from the Fringes may explain Joseph's anxiousness to rid the country of deviations. Perhaps there is a non-religious reason for Joseph's fervor; there certainly seems to be a connection between the two men.

Angus Morton's great-horses give the author another chance for satirical criticism of Joseph and the extremes of his religion. Because these horses can do double the work of ordinary animals at less than twice the feed, it is sensible to use them, but Joseph tries to initiate a campaign against them because "they aren't right!" It is a satire of the attempt of Waknuk religion to maintain the status quo, to stagnate the growth and natural progress of mankind.

It is also interesting that the government in Rigo will sanction something as unusual as the great-horses which can be used for profit, although it is very vigorous in checking any other unnatural form of growth.

Some of the last elements of the background are filled in. Most of preceding history is a convenient blur, so that all the reader needs to know is that the story takes place in what used to be called Labrador, and that David's world is gradually pushing back the frontiers and barbarism created by Tribulation.

An interesting device in the author's style occurs in this chapter. Since the story is told from a first person point of view, everything must inevitably come from David. Instead of giving straight background, which would be quite dull, David explains the world to Sophie, who is ignorant of the facts of her surroundings. Thus, the author completes the details plausibly and interestingly.

The teaching of Ethics clarifies, at least partially, the feelings of Waknuk people toward deviants. If Tribulation was a visitation of God's anger, and if the return to Grace means keeping the human race pure, then it is conceivable that their attempts to maintain purity would often be extreme. This, however, only *explains* their actions, it does not *justify* them.

Glossary

helve: the handle of an axe

sub judice: a case that is still before the court, awaiting a ruling, is said to be *sub judice*

spinney: a small area of brush or undergrowth

ethics: a set of moral principles stating how men must act

attested pedigrees: certified documents signed by witnesses to prove genuine the ancestral line of an animal

rick: a large stack, as of hay

dissemble: pretend

demise: discontinuance or ending of operation

peroration: concluding part of a speech

rectitude: uprightness; goodness, morality

pedant: a person who makes a display of his learning

trenchant: sharp, mentally alert, keen

CHAPTER 5

Discovery and Flight

Summary

It was during an otherwise encouraging season that Sophie was finally exposed. There had been few deviations in the spring-born animals, and the crops were quite normal. Everyone was quite content and, therefore, no one seemed to notice David's frequent absences. It was his custom to hide after the noonday meal and, then, disappear to play with Sophie near her home.

On the day of the discovery David and Sophie were catching shrimp-like creatures in a nearby stream. David, of course, had removed his shoes and, finally, Sophie could not resist the temptation to remove hers as well. It was then that Alan Ervin came along. Although Sophie disappeared immediately, she left a clearly deviant footprint behind. When Alan discovered it, David tackled him, but the blacksmith's son was older and heavier and soon was beating David. The outcome might have been disastrous, but Sophie ended the fighting by dispatching Alan with a rock.

The damage was done. Sophie had been seen, and the Wenders had to flee. David wanted to go, too, but that was impossible. He did stay overnight at the Wender's cottage, however, and crept back to Waknuk the following morning to find the inspector there, and Joseph in one of his more uncontrollable rages. Alan had told on Sophie, and only David's confirmation was needed. It didn't come easily. Finally Joseph whipped him, and Sophie's deviation was forcibly confirmed.

Commentary

David's character is delineated and emphasized more completely here than at any place before. He reveals himself to be at the crucial stage of boy-man, having characteristics of both stages.

Very much the man, he keeps cool when Alan Ervin arrives, and shows quick thinking when he spills water on the footprint. His courage shows when he tackles Ervin, despite the older boy's advantage in height and weight. Yet, like a boy, he almost fails to hold back the tears when the Wenders leave; alone at night in the Wenders' cottage, he is terrified, and tears of self-disgust and humiliation soak his pillow after Joseph beats him.

Nevertheless, David's predominant characteristics show him to be strong and capable, factors he will need if his society should ever "discover" him.

There is both irony and pathos in the exposing of Sophie. It is ironic that Sophie should be discovered in a "good" season. Perhaps if the crops and newborn animals had been deviant, Waknuk probably would not have had time to bother with a simple extra toe. The pathos lies in the fact that such pleasant and likeable people as the Wenders should have to leave their home for a ridiculous reason.

Although the inspector again proves to be quite a humane man, David's father is now the greatest threat to the boy's survival, and the inspector will have to do his job if David is ever found out. At any rate, there is some suspense raised here, because David has harbored knowledge of a deviant without reporting it.

CHAPTER 6
A Geography Lesson from Uncle Axel

Summary

When David calmed down, Rosalind and the others questioned him in thought patterns about what had happened. David explained about Sophie and stated his position that she was not a deviate. They were quite shocked. The teachings of Waknuk were too strong, and they could not accept David's premise.

When David finally slept that night, he dreamt of the city again, and was soothed. But morning brought the inspector, and David was questioned once more about Sophie. Although the boy had, in fact, committed a crime by concealing information, the inspector felt that Joseph had inflicted enough punishment, and omitted David's name in his report. Just after he told David what he had done, Joseph entered to tell them the Wenders had been caught.

A few days later, David, very upset, told Uncle Axel of his plan to run away to the Fringes. This prompted Axel to give a long but logical explanation of why David should not go. His experience as a sailor had taken him to all kinds of Fringes and Badlands country. He had sailed south down the coast, where life forms were so divergent that they could not be defined in terms that Waknuk society would understand. He told David of people in far-off places who tolerated deviations in all life forms. Other people, deviant by Waknuk terms, thought "normal" types to be deviates. In short, according to Axel, the world was not all like Waknuk.

Ultimately, Axel's description led to a private feeling of his own—that, because the Definition of Man came not from the Bible, but from *Nicholson's Repentances*, which had been written *after* the Tribulation, who can say *what* a normal man is? David had always been taught that the True Image of God was man as he was known in Waknuk. Axel's statements began to cast doubt on this supposition. When Axel added that David and Rosalind, because of their peculiar ability, might be closer to the True Image of God than anyone, David shocked his uncle by telling him that there were others besides Rosalind and himself. There were, in fact, six others. They had been nine in number but one, a boy from a distant farm, had been silent for over a month. Axel promised to investigate this silence with a discreet inquiry, and again warned his nephew to be cautious, and to think about the True Image.

Commentary

Axel's enlightening of David is a vital part of this chapter. Principally, Axel is used here as a mouthpiece for the author's own commentary on the belief and behavior of Waknuk. The most important part of this account is his statement that the Definition of Man is from the *Repentances* and not the Bible. Consequently, there is no way of knowing what the True Image of God is. Because the people of Waknuk say a thing is so does not prove it so. Again, the author is satirizing the narrow-mindedness of the community. The people resist change, and hunt down deviations without fully realizing that there is no proof of what actually is normal. Their sin, as far as Axel is concerned, rests not only in the fact that they do not think about their situation but, also, in the fact that they will not let themselves think about it. The people of Waknuk could, themselves, be deviations, and their unthinking certainty that they are right upsets Axel.

The account also includes the discoveries of Marther, an explorer of the lands to the south of Waknuk. This adds more satire because Marther has discovered a truth, that the Fringes can be made fertile and be reclaimed. Yet, because this truth runs counter to the beliefs of Waknuk society, there is agitation for a ban on further exploration. Obviously, there is a suppressed fear that, somehow, they just might be wrong.

Above all, Axel's explanations open David's eyes to the truth about deviation and normalcy. David, who tends to be open-minded, anyway, is given real food for thought—food that may someday nurture his mind if ever he is discovered.

The author fills in the last necessary piece of background to complete the sketch of David's world. This time, he uses Axel to supply the information—a logical choice, since David is obviously too young and inexperienced to know all these things. Then, too, Axel is the only one who would have known or, at any rate, accepted, many of these facts.

There is a slight touch of irony in the fact that David's telepathic associates find it difficult to agree with his acceptance of Sophie. Although they are, in effect, deviates themselves, they are so thoroughly conditioned to believe the True Image that they cannot accept deviancy in another!

The character of the inspector is in strong contrast to that of Joseph. He is kind, and tries to be understanding with David. However, his weakness is demonstrated when, in answer to David's questions, he hides behind the Definition of Man. This behavior may explain to some degree the strength of religion's grip on Waknuk. (That is, of course, Waknuk's own peculiar brand of religion.) Apparently, those people who find the laws of deviancy somewhat harsh are either lacking in intelligence or lacking in strength to argue against them. Consequently, the bigots, like Joseph Strorm, hold power simply because they have tradition and their own strength of personality on their side.

David's dream of a strange city on a big, blue bay begins to take on symbolic value. It seems to create, for him, a kind of paradise where neither deviates nor bigots exit.

The capture of the Wenders, Axel's explanations and warnings, and Joseph's unreasonable fury seem to point to inevitable disaster for David.

Glossary
abetting a concealment: helping to hide a deviate

saprophytes: organisms that live off dead matter

Badlands: Waknuk's name for country that was so affected by Tribulation that it was believed to be unreclaimable, or totally beyond hope of ever supporting life

CHAPTER 7
A Baby and a False Image

Summary

The birth of a baby girl threw the entire Strorm household into a state of tension. Despite the obvious howls of the newborn, no one would acknowledge its existence until the inspector issued a certificate of normalcy. Only when this happened did everyone rejoice.

But the delight that came with the birth of Petra or, at least, with the awarding of the certificate, contrasted with the ugliness of a situation that occurred almost immediately after. David's Aunt Harriet, his mother's sister, appeared in Waknuk one day with a small bundle. Unseen by anyone, she sneaked up a back stairway to the nursery and, there, revealed to Ellen Strorm the contents of the little bundle. She, too, had a little baby girl who had a deviation, just a slight one, but enough to deny her a certificate. Harriet's proposal was to exchange baby girls for a few days until both babies held normalcy certificates. Petra would have served twice, and two children would have survived instead of just one.

But the influence of Joseph was strong. Although Ellen could sense the mother-love, she could not conceal her shock—or her righteousness. Even though she, herself, had given birth to two successive deviates just prior to Petra, she would not accept Harriet's proposal; in fact she launched into a sermon worthy of Joseph, and screamed at her sister for bringing a "monster" into the house. Then, as though Harriet's punishment was not sufficient, Joseph appeared. When he learned the details, Harriet again suffered a verbal beating for her unforgivable sin. Defeated, she left quietly the way she had come. The next day, when her body was found in the river, no one mentioned a baby.

Commentary

This chapter provides the ultimate comment on the society in which David lives. No event (at least in literature) is happier than when a baby is born. Yet for a whole day, with the baby's noises ringing in their ears, the Strorm household pretends that little Petra didn't exist. Had the inspector not issued a certificate this attitude would have continued, and little Petra would have disappeared without ever having been acknowledged. The pathos of Harriet's situation not only underscores this, but her suicide points out the results of such thinking.

It is Harriet's parting statement that reveals this world to be one with no charity, one in which prayers are offered for wrong reasons, one in which religion distorts rather than helps. The author's use of paralleled situations is an effective, if perhaps, heavy-handed way of pointing out the results of Waknuk's beliefs.

An interesting point of character revelation occurs here, also. David's mother, although she clearly objected to Harriet's request, cries when Harriet leaves. Joseph, of course, keeps up his tiresome moralizing through the tears of both women.

Structurally, the story has been to this point, a series of incidents involving or surrounding David, each revealing the unbending morality of Waknuk, and the ridiculousness of its philosophy. Since the climax of these incidents is reached with the death of Harriet and her baby, something inevitably must happen to David.

CHAPTER 8

A Rusted Mirror—Axel Has Doubts

Summary

The death of Aunt Harriet and her baby had disturbed David far more than anything had previously. Perhaps it was because David was one of the few people who knew the reason for her suicide but, more likely, it was because her death brought home to David the realization that he could be a mutant, that, by the rules of his district and his people, he was a Blasphemy and an affront to the True Image.

Uncle Axel noticed the change in David and questioned him. When David recounted the story of Aunt Harriet, and admitted his own fears, Axel began again to expound his own views. He pointed out once more that the Old People were not perfect, that they may not have been the true image at all, and they must have done something quite seriously wrong to bring down such a disaster on the world.

Axel did his best to point out that much of man's development is evolutionary, and that David's society was putting religious tags on factors of life they could not otherwise explain. He emphasized to David that the only thing that distinguished man from other life forms was his mind. David, because he had an extraordinary ability with his mind, should feel gifted rather than feel himself a deviate. David didn't understand all that Axel said but, at least, he felt reassured.

That evening he told the others, six in number besides David and Rosalind, of the conversation. They were Michael, about three miles away, Sally and Katherine, on neighboring farms about two miles away, Mark, nine miles to the west, and Anne and Rachel, sisters, living very close to David.

Michael was sent to school in Kentak and what he learned he sent to the others. Since his education was certainly more liberal than anything David learned, Michael's statements made the group think about their situation, drawing them ever closer together. They were able to carry on this way, undetected, for the next six years.

Commentary

Once again Axel is used as a mouthpiece to explain the author's views and to prepare the readers for future possibilities. He explains that Waknuk people have given religious names and religious significance to things that probably had nothing to do with God at all. Since Tribulation was insane, it could not have been sent by God who must be sane. Thus, though Tribulation covered half of the world, it surely was a man-made thing.

Axel's statements place David in a new light, too. After a brief discussion of evolution, he points out that since the mind distinguishes man from other creatures and, since David and his friends have a higher form of mind, they are likely closer to the True Image than anyone!

A note of hope arises here from the uniqueness of David and his associates. Perhaps they will someday set the world aright. But, Axel's explanation is also a guarantee that, sooner or later, David and company will be in conflict with Waknuk, for Waknuk would never tolerate such a dangerous deviation.

The fact that Tribulation occurs to a lesser degree in Labrador indicates, again, that it was probably nuclear. It is likely that Labrador would not have come under direct attack, and would have suffered minimally compared to the eastern seaboard of North America.

Another view of Waknuk parents is given in the case of Michael. The fact that his mother and father send him to the school in Kentak, because they are not satisfied with the education he would receive in Waknuk, shows that all households are not like the Strorm's.

The success and permanence of the type of religion in the district depends upon people doing little or no thinking. David is forced to think because of his peculiar ability; he has to justify his existence to himself in the light of what he has been taught. It is only natural, then, that he would begin to question the traditional beliefs.

Because the style of this novel frequently leans toward long sermons—by both sides, the author must always keep certain items of suspense before the reader. In this chapter, it is the anticipation of another member for the group; in a previous chapter, it is the sudden silence of another member of the group. But the long-range suspense still originates from the fact that David's deviation must inevitably be discovered. It is this fact that keeps the whole story coherent.

Glossary

poker-work texts: the practice of burning sayings or proverbs into wood or leather. These were the signs that hung in David's home.

funking: shrinking back because of fear or uncertainty

fruition: state of bearing fruit; hence, realization, as in one's hopes or plans

CHAPTER 9

Old Jacob's Views, and a Problem

Summary

Petra joined the group with a terrifying flash one summer afternoon. David was harvesting in a field when a demanding thought pattern struck his mind with such force that it caused him physical pain. Its power made him run several hundred yards toward a stream. On the way, he saw Rosalind running with the same urgency. Only when he dove into a deep pool and rescued Petra did the pain leave his mind.

The cheery little blond girl, it seemed, could create thought patterns with more power than any of them. She had the ability to command. As a six-year-old, though, she had little ability to control her thoughts; nor did she fully realize what her power was or, even, that she had it. In her fear of drowning, she had simply bowled over the others with her panic.

Now the group had a problem. Petra was too young to be aware of her uniqueness, much less her power. Consequently, she was a danger to the group. On the one hand, her power could possibly create a situation that might expose them; on the other, she, herself, might reveal them as deviations. They decided, nevertheless, to forego explaining anything to her until she was old enough to understand. All they could do was hope she wouldn't inadvertently cause a disaster.

Because the group had matured a great deal since the birth of Petra, they had begun to view their society with a great deal more insight. They now knew their predicament. They knew they were not "norms," and that the constant threat of danger was beside them. To compound their difficulties, Petra had revealed herself during a particularly bad season. This season and the previous one had been full of deviations in crops and animals, and people were on edge. They were becoming less and less tolerant of concealments, and more and more willing to search for scapegoats to blame for the visitation of God's wrath.

The feelings of the community were summed up in a conversation David had with Old Jacob. As one of the elder citizens of Waknuk, Jacob represented the more extreme element of the community's philosophy. After talking to him,

David saw clearly what would happen if ever he and his friends were caught.

But Petra didn't reveal them, and things seemed to settle back to a normal pattern. Then Anne announced she was going to marry.

Commentary

Petra's membership in the group adds several new dimensions to the story. The most obvious point is that her thought patterns are more powerful than any of the others. She can also command. Her abilities leave the story open to all kinds of developments. Of more immediate concern, however, is the suspense that arises from the fact that she is too young to realize what she has, and may expose herself and all the others.

There is a change in David. He is older now—sixteen or more, and his maturity is shown. This is seen in his adultlike, analytical description of Petra and the joy she brought to their home. He works in the fields now with the other men. He is also more reflective, and aware of his uniqueness in a society that forbids such an attribute. Above all, his awareness of danger has increased.

Michael's statement that the stupidest "norm" is happier than they are further establishes him as one of the leader-philosophers of the group. It is a bitter but intelligent statement that points out the discomfort felt by anyone who is different from those around him, especially if that difference is unacceptable.

Old Jacob represents the extreme right wing of Waknuk religion. As an old man, he no doubt has witnessed more deviations than others for he has seen the district being settled. Thus, he advocates more rigorous treatment of any aberrations in nature. His reasoning—"Is a tiger-cat responsible for being a tiger-cat? But you kill it!"—shows what chance David and his friends have if they ever have to debate their position.

Jacob shows, too, the feelings of the district during a "bad" season, and the need people have for scapegoats, since they cannot explain things logically.

A device of style common to the novel, occurs again in this chapter. For emphasis, the author frequently juxtaposes two incidents that make each other seem worse simply because they occur together. In this case, it is Jacob's conversation with

David, coming right after the discovery of Petra. In a previous chapter, the joy of Petra's birth offers strong contrast to the sorrow of Harriet and her baby.

Another point of style is the use of dreams; they contribute to the coherence of the novel. Also, David's dream seems to have a special significance that may be revealed later.

Glossary

echelon: an arrangement of men in a series of rows, but patterned like steps

stooking: arranging sheafs of grain into mounds for drying and curing

CHAPTER 10

Love, Marriage, Murder, Suicide

Summary

The others realized the danger inherent in Anne's marrying a "norm," danger not only to Anne, but to themselves as well. They tried to dissuade her, pointing out that to marry someone like they were, would be like trying to marry someone who spoke a different language. She would constantly be disguising her peculiar ability and all of them already knew what that was like, for they had to do it in their own homes.

But Anne's will held. She maintained that, because there were not enough males in the group, two of the girls would always have to remain unwed and lonely and this, she said, was not going to happen to her. Thus, she married Alan Ervin, the man who, years before, had turned in Sophie Wender.

Her marriage pointed up the developing relationship between David and Rosalind. They, too, were drifting toward marriage, but their difficulties were different. The disagreements of their fathers had grown into open feud and any meeting of the two lovers had to be very discreet.

David's discussion with Axel about the problem with Anne merely increased the worry over the marriage. Axel pointed out that sooner or later Anne would expose the group. As a woman in love, he said, she would want to share everything with her husband; the group's days were numbered. But Axel also posed another query to David. He questioned whether one person had the moral right to endanger the lives of the majority, but David balked at the thought of murder.

Anne, meanwhile, had shut off her mind to the rest of the group. She neither gave nor received any thought patterns for the first six months of her marriage. Then one evening Alan Ervin was found dead with an arrow through his neck.

The group panicked. Nor were they soothed by Anne's refusal to see Rachel, her own sister. Naturally, they feared that Anne suspected one of them was the murderer; and their fears were true.

When Anne was not seen around her house, Rachel forced her way in, and found her sister hanging from a beam in the bedroom. She also found a note listing the names of the entire group, including Rachel—and it was addressed to the inspector.

The relief at Rachel's discovering the note was unbounded but, as Michael pointed out, the entire incident showed what could happen when one of them was not strong enough.

Commentary

Unquestionably, the marriage of Anne to a "norm" is the most important part of Chapter 10. It is important because, for the first time, a member of the group denies their common welfare, and commits herself outside the group. The fact that they are not exposed is due only to the coincidence of Rachel's finding the note, and the intervention of a well-placed arrow. Michael voices the obvious conclusion when he comments that one of them has not been strong enough.

David and Rosalind are in love but, ironically, although they don't have Anne's problem, they face a difficulty that any pair of norms could face—feuding families.

Axel underlines the seriousness of the group's dilemma when he suggests that one could be prevented from endangering the many.

The maturity of David's thinking comes to the fore when he tells Axel he would rather have a sword hanging over him, than burning inside him.

CHAPTER 11

The Education of Petra

Summary

The following spring held promise of a good year. There were practically no deviations at all, and people began to look toward harvest time with optimism. It was during this spring that Petra, now eight and a half, decided to demonstrate her power again.

Petra had broken a family rule, and was riding alone in the West Woods when she was attacked. A wildly deviant creature killed her pony and she was forced into a treetop for safety. The result, of course, was Petra's panicked but overpowering call for help. The first one to arrive was David but, even as he unlimbered his gun, an arrow pierced the creature's throat, followed by two more in rapid succession. Behind him, Rosalind and Michael came riding out of the bushes. As the three of them tried to calm Petra with soothing thought patterns, Rachel and Mark came riding in. The compelling nature of Petra's call was evident here, for David had never seen Mark before.

Calming Petra was impossible for the time at least and, lest they all be seen together and arouse suspicion, Michael, Rachel and Mark rode away. Yet, no sooner had they disappeared when Sally and Katherine came riding into the clearing and, on their heels, was a stranger who looked suspicious to David.

The man's name was Joseph Skinner, and he was plainly wary of the group before him. Spies from the Fringes, and rumored raids had made people very cautious. He was particularly curious about how they all knew where to go, especially since he had seen Sally and Katherine gallop away suddenly, but he had not heard what they claimed to have heard. David was disturbed by the fact that the man seemed to doubt their explanations, but the more immediate problem was Petra's terrified grip on everyone's brain. So strong was her pattern that none of them could communicate with the others.

It was only that night, when Petra fell asleep, that the bonds loosened, and the group was able to discuss what to do about her.

They decided it was time to explain to Petra the powers she possessed. This task David undertook the following afternoon on a fishing trip. It was very difficult at first for, as soon as Petra realized that she could consciously communicate in thought patterns, she literally knocked everyone off their feet. Gradually though, she began to understand the nature of her power, but not the extent of it. Within a month she was sending out crude but relatively controlled images.

Her vast power opened a fascinating new possibility, for she had apparently established contact with others far beyond the Waknuk group. But either she could not understand them, or else she was not able to convey the meaning of their patterns. Petra was destined for an unknown and exciting future.

Uncle Axel again came into the picture with shocking news. He had noticed David worrying and questioned him. When David explained the incident with Petra, his uncle surprised him by saying that he already knew that Petra was one of the group. His experience in life had made him suspicious of Alan Ervin, and close observation of Anne's husband had led him to the conclusion that the group's safety was in jeopardy. It was Axel who had killed Alan Ervin.

Things seemed to be getting worse, especially because of Skinner. In David's district, too, there were inquiries. Therefore, Michael proposed the plan that Sally and Katherine arrange to escape together whenever the time came, and that David, Rosalind and Petra do the same.

Commentary

The group is unquestionably in trouble now, and their detection is imminent. The suspense now depends more on the question of who will be caught, and how, rather than if they will be caught. Even though they are older now and capable of debating their position, previous actions by the people of Waknuk show that any kind of argument would be futile.

Petra's power is again demonstrated by the fact that she is able to bring the group together in spite of itself. But her power introduces another level of plot for the story. She apparently contacts thought projectioners from a society far beyond the district of Waknuk.

Character is delineated in this chapter. Michael's cool leadership qualities are shown when he takes over the planning and advising. David's humanity and kindness are evident in his patient teaching of Petra.

Axel's curious loyalty is seen in his murder of Alan Ervin. Axel is really a special case in this novel. He is so distinct from other citizens of Waknuk—reflective, philosophical, intelligent, and practical to the point of killing Alan Ervin as the least of possible evils. Despite his murder of Anne's husband, he is not an immoral or irreligious man. Yet his act of murder is almost a frustrated contribution to the cause of David's group. It is indicative of the helplessness that one must feel if he opposes the Waknuk philosophy. It is all that Axel can do!

The punishment of deviates is clearly revealed for the first time here. If any of the group are caught, they will be sterilized, and banished to the Fringes. This, no doubt, accounts for the stealing of babies in raids from the Fringes.

Glossary

orthodoxy: sound and correct opinion; in this case, correct qualities

amorphous splodge: shapeless splotch

retroussé: turned-up

tribunal: a court of justice; in this case, a court which rules on deviations

propitious: favorable, promising

abeyance: a condition of suspended activity

proprietorial: arising from or showing awareness of ownership

overt: open; not secret

CHAPTER 12

The Flight to the Fringes

Summary

Michael's proposals frightened David, and he fell asleep planning the items he should pack in the next few days in case an emergency really did happen. His sleep was soon interrupted, and Petra was awake. Rosalind had come through. They had taken Sally and Katherine. Rosalind said she would wait for them by the mill, but David and Petra would have to come immediately. The two sneaked to the stable, mounted Sheba, and stole quietly away as the sound of approaching horses came to their ears.

They arrived at the mill to find Rosalind waiting with the great-horses and plenty of supplies. She explained that her mother had learned of their deviation and had helped her prepare. Mrs. Morton, apparently, had half-known all along that there was something different about her daughter. This made David think about his mother—whether she would have helped him or whether she even suspected her children weren't really "norms."

Suddenly, Michael burst through. Planning ahead as usual, he said that he was going to join one of the posses, since neither he nor Rachel nor Mark were suspect. He would initiate a rumor that the fugitives were heading southeast. When this proved false, Mark was to suggest the northwest. This would make time for the great-horses to plod even further to the southwest before the true trail was discovered.

David awoke from their first rest to find Rosalind terribly upset. The first victim of the chase had fallen. While Rosalind had stood watch, a man had approached and she had killed him with an arrow. Michael said it—it was war.

The second victim was heard from shortly after. Katherine had broken under torture, and Sally had yielded, too. Sally apologized tearfully for what she had done. Katherine couldn't communicate. As it stood now, David, Rosalind and Petra were officially branded as outlaws, although Michael, Rachel and Mark were still unsuspected. The new brand meant, however, the the fugitives could be killed on sight without penalty. Michael added to this chilling information the fact that the people of Waknuk wanted to catch them very badly. They were deviates who had been deceiving the district for years and represented a real threat to Waknuk's way of life. For David, this meant that the Wild Country would not be safe enough even on a temporary basis; they would have to head for the Fringes.

This terrified Petra and they spent the next half hour trying to soothe her. She had been told horrible stories of the Fringes when she was a small child and she was still too young to have forgotten them. But Petra had received some more thought shapes again. These came from very far away. The distant thought-people wanted to know what had upset her so.

Petra did her best to translate the messages from these distant people, but the best that David and the others could decipher was that the thoughts came from a place called Sealand or Zealand. Part of the message apparently included a description of a marvellous city with beautiful buildings, fish-shaped flying things and carts without horses. It was David's dream!

But the peculiar transmission of thoughts had to be forgotten for the moment. The posse had discovered their trail, and as the great-horses were urged to a trot, they came face to face with another horseman.

Commentary

David's group is finally in open conflict with the district of Waknuk. As a matter of fact, as Michael put it, they are at war. The group presents a threat that goes beyond the problem of the True Image. Because they are telepathic, they could infiltrate and overthrow the ruling bodies of Waknuk before these people could know what had happened. Thus, in a sense, it was war to the people of Waknuk, too, not just a search for escaped deviates.

Further proof of the reality of war is demonstrated when Rosalind kills, and when Katherine is tortured. This torture, too, indicates to what extent the people of Waknuk will go to achieve their ends. But perhaps it shows their fear even more.

Mrs. Morton's assistance raises the question for David of how many mothers conceal deviates. It indicates that human love might overcome the thirst for purity that makes Waknuk such a terrible place to live.

The resourcefulness and coolness of Rosalind is given its first display in this chapter. She makes an excellent partner for David and lends hope to the possibility of their escape.

Again Petra receives messages from far off—so far off that the others cannot grasp them. This time, however, they are more distinct and meaningful. Thus, a new element has been introduced into the story. One wonders just who these people are, and what they have to do with the story, especially since they have a connection with David's childhood dream.

Glossary

Sealand: probably what we know as New Zealand

spoor: trail or track

hobble the horses: tie or fasten their legs together loosely so that they can graze, but not run away

imminent: threatening to occur immediately

CHAPTER 13
Message from Sealand

Summary

After an exchange of shots, the group succeeded only in wounding the man's horse. They escaped, but they had left behind them clear evidence of where they were.

After riding a few miles more, the vegetation showed that they had reached the Wild Country. They clumped through a farm without interference, and stopped to rest in a clearing just beyond.

Suddenly, Petra knocked them out again with one of her blinding communications. The Sealand people, she said, wanted to talk to David and Rosalind. But communication for them was still impossible and Petra was forced to translate in her childlike way.

The message was that Petra was to be protected at all costs. Sealand people were coming to rescue the fugitives, but they were principally interested in Petra because of her amazing powers of transmission.

The others were not sure how to treat this bit of surprising information. They, too, knew that Petra was exceptional, but they gave little weight to the possibility that anyone might be coming to their rescue. And of more immediate concern, Michael came through with the information that the posse had picked up the trail again and it was time to move on. Michael added that Sally and Katherine weren't coming through any more and that, if the fugitives were captured, David should kill Rosalind and Petra rather than let them be captured alive.

Petra was more curious than frightened and in her childish innocence, asked why they were being pursued. David could only answer that it was because people could not stand others different from themselves.

As they pushed on, Petra's strange friends kept up the communication and, as the dialogue developed, there were indications that they considered theirs a superior civilization to that in Waknuk.

But all time for conjecture of this type disappeared when a gunshot caused the horses to bolt out of control. When they finally slowed to a walk, they were well into Fringes country. It was here that David was struck unconscious.

Commentary

Petra takes on a special importance once more because of her extraordinary powers in thought transmission. It is this that the Sealand people are primarily interested in, and it is because of her power that they show concern for the fugitives.

Although David thinks little of Sealand's intentions to rescue them, there are indications that theirs is a vastly superior culture. Apparently, everyone there can make thought patterns, and there is no thought that this might be a deviation.

David tries to explain to Petra why they are running for their lives. His explanation is again a vehicle of satire for the author. Because they are different, he tells Petra, they cause the people of Waknuk to feel insecure and afraid. As he says, it is a "feel-thing" not a "think-thing," and the more stupid people are, the more they feel everyone should be the same. It is an interesting consideration that the author is not only pointing out a flaw in Waknuk society, he is telling us something about our own, too.

Glossary

disembowelled: torn open so the bowels come out

sententiously: speaking as if one were a judge settling a question

CHAPTER 14
The Spider-Man

Summary

When David regained consciousness, he was in the familiar basket of one of the great-horses, but his thumbs were neatly tied together. Rosalind and Petra were in the same situation, but in another basket.

As they penetrated farther into the Fringes, David expressed his astonishment at the degree of deviation in the vegetation. His captor answered this, expressing his faith that it would get better—as soon as God's little game of patience was over. This shocked David—not the philosophy, for Axel had explained that—but the Fringes man's reference to God. David had always been taught that the Fringes had been inspired by Satan and that he was worshipped there. This prompted the captor into a long exposition of his view of Tribulation, deviation and recovery. It was, understandably enough, a justification of the Fringes and its people, and a condemnation of Waknuk and its beliefs.

But David tried to steer away from a theological argument and tried to concern himself with their immediate fate. Since they were physically normal, they would have to explain their presence by revealing at least a part of their powers. The group consulted and decided to tell their captors as little as possible, but to reveal, certainly, that they were the objects of an intense pursuit. This latter point didn't seem to bother the Fringes men at all.

At this point the Sealand lady came through. But now she was close enough for the others to pick up. Since Petra was no longer needed for translation, the communication was more mature. The Sealand lady began to philosophize on deviations, the Old People, and their own telepathic ability. She explained the good fortune of her country in avoiding much of Tribulation, and again emphasized the importance of maintaining Petra's safety.

Because the Sealand people lived on two islands far to the south, they had partially escaped Tribulation. During the recovery period, somehow the think-together strain began and developed. As Sealand civilization improved they were able to build machines and, eventually, make rescue attempts of other think-together people. This explained their effort to save the fugitives.

Finally, the group arrived at the Fringes. The settlement was a collection of hovels and refuse heaps. When David was taken to the leader, his face froze in shock. It was the captive he had seen years before at Waknuk—Joseph Storm's elder brother!

The man questioned David and discovered that a posse of over a hundred men had followed them into the Fringes. This betrayal of his former neighbors didn't bother David as much as the Spider-Man, who was looking hungrily at Rosalind. David's frustration at this grew until he tackled the man, but he was beaten senseless for his efforts.

Commentary

This is a chapter of crisis. David, Rosalind and Petra flee from Waknuk to escape prosecution and, most likely, execution. Their one area of safety is the Fringes. Now they are in an equally difficult predicament. Their hope is that the Fringes people will accept them or, at least, leave them alone. But now they are captives; David fought with their leader and lies unconscious, and the leader obviously desires Rosalind.

Not only is there suspense concerning the safety of the fugitives, the romantic interest develops a great deal as well. By clearly establishing David's feelings for Rosalind, the author creates a stronger desire in the reader for a happy outcome. Thus, the anxiety about their current predicament is intensified.

The Sealand woman's explanation of her country is both important to the story and interesting to twentieth-century readers. That New Zealand would escape the worst effects of a nuclear holocaust is a theory that many scientists accept today. The novel consequently is made even more believable.

The Sealand philosophy is best summed up in the woman's reply to David's question. When he asks if they are the kind of people God intended, she replies, "I don't know about that. Who does?" It is this kind of thinking that the author, both subtly and openly, advocates throughout the novel. There is obviously an indication here that if the conflict in this novel is to be resolved, it will be done through the agency of these Sealand people.

David's conversation with his rather articulate Fringes captor serves a dual purpose. It is, again, a satirical comment on Waknuk's theories of deviation for, as the man says, the most productive and superior breeds are selected as normal. But his comments also reveal a kind of thinking that smacks very much of Waknuk itself. The Fringes people, too, have a theory of deviation and the cause of Tribulation. The irony is that this theory about God and themselves is almost as narrow as that of the society of Waknuk. The only difference is in approach.

What this occasion teaches David is that his own well-being, and that of mankind, would be no better off in the hands of these people than in the control of men like Joseph Strorm. It also indicates to the reader that something further must develop, since the rescue of David and the others does not lie here.

More satire or, perhaps, bitter comment is given through the Sealand woman. This time it is directed at twentieth-century society. She points out the Old People's inability to live together in large units—a rather unique way to phrase a historical analysis of our current wars.

The background of the Spider-Man who, in other circumstances, would be the owner of Joseph Strorm's farm, might account in part for the latter's extreme position on deviation. There is a suggestion that Joseph has guilt feelings and that, by stamping out all deviations in Waknuk, he is justifying his ownership of the farm and the fate of his brother.

One of the author's peculiarities of style is evident, again, in this chapter. He frequently uses a minor character to act as a mouthpiece for his views (e.g., the Fringes captor, the Sealand lady and Axel) but, in order that this sermonizing should fit logically into the story, these long passages are usually in response to David's naïve questions or arguments.

Glossary

    symbiosis: a blending into one; close association
    aberrate: to deviate from the normal
    miscegenate: a mixture of types
    homogeneal: of a similar kind or nature
    consensus: agreement in opinion

CHAPTER 15
Sophie

Summary

When David recovered he found himself in the care of Sophie. Immediately, he made sure that Rosalind and Petra were all right. They were asleep, and quite safe, and the Spider-Man was gone, leading an expedition against the invaders.

As David quickly explained why he was here in the Fringes, and why he was in this particular predicament, it appeared that he and Sophie shared a similar worry. Sophie was the Spider-Man's wife and, while David worried about the man's desire for Rosalind, Sophie feared losing him because Rosalind could bear children, and she couldn't. For the sake of everyone, however, there had to be an escape. Sophie took David to her quarters to arrange it.

While this was going on, the Sealand woman sent a thought message to say that she and her rescue party were only sixteen hours away. Michael came in, worried because he had not heard from Mark and Rachel who were still in Waknuk. As yet, he said, their party had not met the Fringes men, but they expected to do battle before long.

It was just after this exchange that Sophie took a knife and killed the guard.

Commentary

This chapter is very appropriately devoted to Sophie, for it is through her that the author makes some of his most devastating comments about the effects of Waknuk religion. Sophie, who is innocent, cheerful, clean and happy, now lives in the most despairing conditions imaginable simply because of her extra toe.

The Wenders' cottage, which David had thought so pleasant compared to his home, is replaced by a filthy cave. Sophie's appearance changes so that David barely recognizes her. She is the wife of a spiderlike man, but could not even give him children, for the Waknuk officials had sterilized her. Finally, little Sophie could kill! "This is the Fringes," she says.

CHAPTER 16
A Place Among the Fossils

Summary

Sophie's next step was to see that Rosalind and Petra removed their crosses. This particular element of Waknuk tradition was not favorably regarded in the Fringes. The crosses had not served these people very well. Rosalind, of course, hesitated. She had never known any other mode of dress, and years of habit are hard to break in a moment. This slight hesitation capped the buildup of tension in Sophie and she exploded into a rage. In her anger, she admitted her love for David and, also, her frustration because of it. Finally, she fell on the floor sobbing. The rest simply hung their heads, afraid to look at one another.

No one said much after this, and David eventually fell asleep. When he awoke, Michael was calling him. They had met the Fringes army and had defeated them. This meant that the survivors would be retreating to their camp to regroup and David and the others might be discovered.

Petra's Sealand friends, meanwhile, were still on the way, closer than they had thought they would be. They commented, too, on the Badlands they were crossing, asking what kind of hell that Tribulation had brought to this area.

Meanwhile, the suspense increased. The final battle between the Fringes people and the citizens of Waknuk was fast approaching, and David stood a good chance of being caught in the middle. Suddenly, Petra flashed out a thought pattern asking if Joseph was in the advancing army. Michael was unable to disguise his answer. Now David was faced with the alternative of attacking the Fringes men or fighting his own father. Neither foe would be likely to turn away.

But the Sealand woman urged him to forget the problem; she said that Joseph and his kind were like fossils, mere curiosity pieces in the flow of history, and that soon the situation would be just a memory.

A few hours later, Michael was coming through again. The Fringes force, which had needed the element of surprise to be successful, had lost the opportunity for ambush and was in full retreat. The Waknuk posse was almost at the edge of the camp. At that moment, David could see the pitiful retreating deviates, frightened and disorganized, clinging to the Spider-Man for some kind of leadership.

For a few moments they held their own against the superior forces of Waknuk, but a flanking movement threw them into complete disorder. In the midst of the confusion the Spider-Man stood calmly until Joseph Strorm appeared; and then he raised his weapon and shot him through the heart. Turning quickly, he grabbed Sophie and ran, but he took no more than three steps before both of them fell in a hail of arrows.

Suddenly, strange strings of sticky substance began to fall among the combatants, miring them in a viscous mess. Unable to move, they stopped fighting. From above, the ship of the Sealand people began to settle to earth.

Commentary

An era ends with the death of Joseph Strorm. Neither the Fringes, nor Waknuk will be the same again. But for this, Joseph's death is necessary and symbolic. He stands for all that is wrong in the existence of the two districts. His position, and Waknuk's interpretation of mankind, is appropriately labelled in the comment of the Sealand lady. She says that his is an attempt to fix, or arrest, human development and to maintain a single form of human being. The only way to do this is to fossilize it.

Again, the Sealand woman takes on the part of a mouthpiece for the author. In her flight to rescue the fugitives, the comments on extreme Badlands can only deal with the former United States—no doubt a cautious, but satiric warning against nuclear politics.

In the conflict of Sophie and Rosalind, brief as it is, the author toys with something that could have been an addition to the novel, but he never develops it. By having a conflicting love interest over David, things could have been very complicated, indeed, at the end of the story. But a number of factors eliminate this possibility. In the first place, Sophie is chased out of Waknuk before she and David could form a mature, romantic relationship. Also, Sophie is of the "old world," and David is going to Sealand. Then, too, Sophie's humiliating death at the side of the Spider-Man is the final statement of pathos in a very pathetic life story.

Glossary

tableau: sometimes called a living picture; usually, it is a group of people standing transfixed in reaction to some incident

appliqué: an adornment sewn onto a dress

treacle: viscous, sticky substance

CHAPTER 17

A Brave New World

Summary

David lay immobilized by the sticky, gossamer substance. Rosalind and Petra, too, were frozen by it, for the landing of the ship had blown it into the cave. Soon though, they caught Michael's thought pattern of relief, and it wasn't long until they, too, were rescued.

Before them stood a young woman in a glistening white suit. She held a spray that released them from the grasp of the filaments. After brief introductions, she urged that everyone board and take off immediately for Sealand. It was only after this command that the group realized everyone outside was dead, killed by the white substance.

The Sealand woman sermonized briefly, rationalizing their destruction of the combatants. That the Fringes people and the force from Waknuk should die, she said, was inevitable, for the former were so miserable that they had nothing to look forward to, and the latter had foolishly tried to arrest history. Consider, she reminded the group, what either side would have done to them, had the Sealand ship not arrived.

Although this calmed everyone temporarily, the question of taking off was not that simple. Michael would not go because they could not land in Waknuk to pick up Rachel. It was finally agreed that he would return to Waknuk, and the two of them would find their own way to Sealand if they could.

The take off was accomplished without difficulty, and the journey was uneventful but, as they approached the main city of Sealand, David saw what he had been dreaming of as a child. It was his city on the harbor! Everyone was so excited that they forgave Petra for bowling them over with her uncontrollable delight.

Commentary

Stylistically, the final chapter is designed to close the plot of the story, and leave the reader with things to contemplate. This the author hopes to achieve through the Sealand people.

Initially, they bring an end to the novel by destroying the Fringes people and the Waknuk posse. But this kind of mass execution must be explained and justified or the novel will end on as pessimistic a note as it begins. Unless the Sealand people have purpose and direction, their elimination of the others makes them as bad or worse than those they destroy.

The Sealand woman explains this act by saying that the Fringes people have no future but misery; the implication here may be that they are being done a favor. Waknuk tries to impose a freeze on mankind, to arrest evolution. By destroying these people, the implication continues, the Sealand forces are doing mankind a service.

But, the ultimate justification and, perhaps, one that is a little frightening, is the fact that the Sealanders and David's group are superior variants of the human species. As superior beings, they may lead the world and mankind to great heights. The essence of life is change, and they, the Sealand lady says, are a change for the better.

That the "think-together" people are superior in many ways is no doubt true, but it is a little chilling to think that they look upon Waknuk as a "drag" on the human race. Their arbitrary elimination of the two separate forces is a rather disturbing point.

But the happiness of the ending lies in the fact that the hero and his friends are rescued and face a prospect of contentment and peace.

There is hope, too, in the love of Michael for Rachel. The strength of love has always been one of the redeeming qualities of the human race, and Michael's sacrifice for Rachel shows that this has not been lost in the development of a "superior variant."

The great city in Sealand brings the symbolic value of David's dream to its ultimate conclusion and, of course, gives unity to the novel.

Glossary

apologia: a defence or justification of the way one conducts his life

superior variant: a type of species; in this case, a type of human species that is better than others

Character Sketches

David

David's personality is the most completely revealed of all the characters in the novel because he is both the narrator and the hero.

His survival in the family of Joseph Strorm is due, partly, to Uncle Axel's interest in him and to good fortune, but he also survives because of his intelligence and resourcefulness. David thinks about his society and realizes that, by its standards, he is a deviate and is not to be tolerated.

David's bravery is one of his most outstanding characteristics. He first shows courage by tackling Alan Ervin when his attempt to obliterate Sophie's tracks fails to deceive the older boy. His bravery is a contributing factor to the successful escape of the group to the Fringes.

Teaching Petra shows his patience; he handles this difficult task with kindness and concern.

David is a believable character. He yields to his father's punishment and reveals Sophie's deviation. Knowing the sorry consequence that Waknuk society will impose on Sophie and her family because of her abnormality, he plans, through his hot tears, to run away. However, in the midst of his planning and because of his emotional exhaustion, he falls asleep.

Petra

Petra's childish exuberance and enthusiasm is a refreshing contrast to the pervasive gloom of the novel. Unhappily, her overwhelming extrasensory power and her inability to keep it under control combine with her enthusiasm to get the group into trouble.

Sophie

Sophie is one of the few characters in the novel whose personality undergoes a change. Every one of her character traits seems designed to emphasize the pathos of her story.

As a child, she is bright, curious, cheerful and friendly, yet pathetically aware that she is somehow different from everyone else. The enviable traits of her youth contrast with the bitterness she exhibits in the Fringes. This bitterness leads her to become angry, to hate and to kill.

Old Jacob

Surly, complaining, and narrow-minded, Jacob represents all the characteristics of an old man whose bitterness, at everything in general, outweighs whatever humanity survives in him. Jacob's bitter tirade against what he thinks are liberalizing trends in Waknuk shows him to be an ultra-right-wing supporter of the religion. He also represents the opinion of the older, and still surviving, early settlers of the district. Less a character than a caricature, Jacob is a good example of the kind of person who could embrace the philosophy of the community without question. He also, perhaps, explains why the feelings of Waknuk are so intense regarding deviations. As a settler, Jacob has seen more deviations than most people and is, therefore, more anxious to have them stamped out. This is especially so since he spent his early years in the district in an active campaign against abnormal life forms. The second generation in Waknuk (Joseph's) is very likely to have inherited this zeal.

The Inspector

Because the inspector is charged with maintaining the purity of the district, one would expect him to be a cruel and heartless man. Instead, he shows himself to be quite humane in dealing with David. He tries to explain to the boy what must be done to the Wenders, and why. He assures David that their capture is an accident, and not the boy's fault. However, it is this explanation that reveals to David his only other prominent characteristic: he does not think. To David's questions, he merely quotes from *Nicholson's Repentances*. His character here represents the typical Waknuk attitude—hide behind the rules rather than think about them.

Still, on grounds where he can handle himself, the inspector is firm. He opposes Joseph Strorm on several occasions, each time basing his decision on common sense or kindness.

Alan Ervin

On the only occasions we encounter him, Alan is cruel. When he maliciously reports Sophie Wender, he indulges in mere childish cruelty, but Waknuk society turns this into a tragedy. In his defence, however, it could be argued that his childhood cruelty is learned, not natural. Children are taught to expose deviations. Yet, Axel sees the fiendish look in his eye after he marries Anne. Alan learns the truth about some people and does something about it.

Joseph Strorm
Here is the ultimate villain, and victim, of Waknuk philosophy. Because the morality of the community is stern, unrelenting, unthinking and fierce, Joseph Strorm is ideally suited for it, since each of these adjectives applies aptly to him. His characteristics are most horribly demonstrated in dealings with his own family. When he should be most kind, he is cruel. Aunt Harriet, Emily, David, unmentioned babies, and neighbors are all victims of his, from his tiresome sermons to his blind purging of deviants. Joseph is so terrifying and so obnoxious that he is, really, a caricature of the firm believers in Waknuk.

Emily Strorm
David's mother is much like Alan Ervin in that she is an example of what happens to people in Waknuk. Emily denies a softness in herself to follow the hard line of the faith. Her tears at Harriet's predicament reveal her true softness, but her harsh criticism of her sister shows how thoroughly she succumbs to her husband and his beliefs.

Harriet Strorm
Another victim of both Joseph and Waknuk, Harriet shows a streak of defiance in her answer to her tormentor and in her suicide. However, her soft mother-love for a deviant child shows the reader what feelings do exist in Waknuk—feelings that are suppressed and not mentioned.

Angus Morton
Angus's ownership of the great-horses indicates that he is probably broad-minded and intelligent. His presence in the novel is evidence of a progressive element in Waknuk.

Uncle Axel
Clearly the most intellectual of David's acquaintances, Uncle Axel understands the driving forces in Waknuk. Although he, himself, is intelligent, analytical and humane, he represents still another factor in Waknuk life for he is helpless

to correct a situation which he knows is wrong. Ironically, the only time he effectively alters conditions in Waknuk is when he commits murder. His morality is of a type that justifies killing one to save the majority.

The Wenders
Sophie's parents are kind, considerate and very realistic. They represent those citizens of Waknuk who quietly defy the system but are, in fact, helpless in the face of it.

Anne
Anne's marriage to Alan Ervin suggests a dangerously unreasonable streak of stubbornness, and her subsequent exposure of the group verifies this shortcoming in her character. Her statement that she will not remain unmarried for the sake of the group indicates her selfishness. Her suicide is no redeeming factor, either, for it is probably the result of frustration, not remorse.

Rosalind
Because Rosalind is David's sweetheart, we receive nothing but favorable impressions of her. Objectively, all one could şay is that she is quite resourceful, and makes an excellent partner for the escape. Yet, her coolness is tempered by a genuine femininity that shows itself in her remorse at having to kill a man during the escape.

Michael
The philosopher of the group, Michael's comments are always incisive and accurate. As a very intelligent person, he makes a very capable leader.

Structure

Because the story is told in the first person, it naturally deals only with those events which affect the hero, David Strorm. The structure or plot of the novel is, therefore, basically an account of the growing up of David from the age of nine or ten until his flight into the Fringes in his middle teens.

As David grows up, he gains increasing knowledge about the world and society in which he lives. Thus, the novel contains large sections of information necessary for both David's education and as background for the reader's understanding of the situation. This information is worked into the novel in the form of discussions between David and certain other characters, particularly, Sophie, Uncle Alex, the group, the Fringe man and the Sealand lady.

Ordinarily, there is a danger that this would be an episodic plot, a series of occurrences that have coherence only because they deal with one person. But a sense of logical development is achieved in *The Chrysalids* by the ever-present threat of danger to David, and the suspenseful awareness that sooner or later he will be exposed. Consequently, the basic structure of the novel consists of the series of events that lead to David's ultimate discovery, flight and rescue.

This basic structure of events traces the movement of David's own self-discovery. He first comes to realize his own difference. Then, this difference is discovered by the others of his society, resulting in the flight of the group and open conflict with Waknuk society. The final section of the novel shows the difference, which had set David and the group apart, become the norm in a new and less enclosed society in Sealand. In this way, the structure of the novel is rescued from being episodic, because each occurrence is part of this movement toward self-discovery and acceptance.

The introduction of the novel carries through to the capture of Sophie Wender, for it is here that David learns of the cruelty of Waknuk. The buildup, or rising action, continues from this point to the crisis, which is Petra's rescue from a deviant beast in the woods. The denouement carries from here to the rescue of the fugitives by the Sealand people. The conclusion is the last chapter, in which David, Rosalind and Petra join their friends in Sealand.

Setting

Historical

The society of Waknuk approximates what we know as the late seventeenth century. It is based on agriculture, with little evidence of any industrialization. Like eighteenth-century England or North America, the people are very provincial in their outlook; their lives are controlled by a rigid code of morality and religious beliefs that are repressive and, often, fierce.

The justification of these standards comes from Tribulation, a phenomenon which they believe was a visitation of God's wrath upon His people or, more specifically, the Old People. The Old People clearly constitute the society of the twentieth century, and the readers of the novel. Frequent references are made to airplanes, automobiles and other twentieth-century inventions.

Ironically, however, the Old People who are held up as an ideal were the ones who were punished by Tribulation which was, in all probability, a nuclear holocaust. The effect of radiation, no doubt, is the cause of all the deviations that afflict David's society.

Paradoxically, then, Waknuk is a society of the future with a setting from the past.

Sealand, on the other hand, seems to have escaped Tribulation to some degree, and has advanced beyond the level of the twentieth century, both in physical setting, and in outlook.

Geographical

Although both Labrador and New Zealand escape nuclear destruction, the similarity ends there. Whereas Sealand is industrial and progressive, Waknuk is agricultural and regressive or, at best, stagnant.

The middle of Labrador is affected by radiation to the extent that its climate is now temperate and suited to agricultural development. The farming appears to be somewhat communal, with one large farm having a great number of dependent workers. Houses are built close together for mutual help and protection.

Although the immediate area is fairly free of deviations, the countryside is full of them. Around Waknuk is the Wild Country, which could be equated with what we know as a frontier. Here, there is little control of nature by man, and all types of deviant forms of life thrive.

The Fringes, which surrounds the Wild Country, contains practically no normal forms of life as we know them, and beyond this belt is a vast area known as the Badlands, where the worst results of radiation are found. Nothing grows; everything is black char. Evidence in the novel indicates that the Badlands are areas of what was once the United States.

Social

The single, dominant fact of life in Waknuk, as David learns in his lessons in Ethics, is the process of climbing back into the grace of God. Tribulation had been a punishment, like expulsion from Eden, the Flood and so on, and the road back to God's favor is not an easy one.

Since there is only one true path and, since this is determined by learned writings such as *Nicholson's Repentances*, only the ecclesiastical and lay authorities could properly rule on what is right and proper. Anything that deviates from what they say is normal has to be destroyed, for it was not only a temptation leading away from the true path, it was, also, an insult directed at God. Above all, mankind's greatest duty is to see that the human form is kept true to the divine pattern.

For guidance, the people of Waknuk could turn to the Bible, which has survived Tribulation but, more often, they turn to *Nicholson's Repentances*. This is a series of lessons written during the age of barbarism, just after Tribulation, and it is the only place where the True Image is described. Consequently, this volume is both a rulebook and a justification for the stern morality of Waknuk.

The normal factors that influence an agricultural community are minor in relation to the power of the religion. Even marriage is affected, for a husband may turn out his wife if she produces three consecutive deviant children.

Because it is so dominant, little else but religion penetrates David's existence as a child.

Atmosphere

In *The Chrysalids*, atmosphere varies extensively. In the first place the reader's curiosity is aroused. There is, of course, the normal interest at the beginning of a novel as the characters reveal themselves, and the plot unfolds. But the stronger curiosity in this novel, no doubt, arises from the urge to identify the society. It is familiar, yet unfamiliar. Just when the reader pinpoints it as belonging to the eighteenth century, somewhere in the Western Hemisphere, a vague reference is given to suggest that this is not so.

Then, there is the peculiarity of the society itself. There is a natural interest in people like ourselves, but these have a different set of beliefs and here, too, there is a suggestion of curiosity.

As the setting, characters and background are established, the atmosphere begins to change to one of fear. This occurs for two reasons. The amazing lack of charity, and unbending set of rules in David's community are frightening in themselves but, by this time, we have come to know and like David and, realizing that he, too, is a deviant, we fear for him.

Several incidents such as the flight of the Wenders, and the suicide of Aunt Harriet, increase this fear. We now anticipate and expect that David will be discovered. When it finally does happen there is almost a sense of relief.

By this time, though, an air of hope is present. Petra's communication with a whole society of "thought-makers" gives some assurance that the fugitives will escape.

It is significant that the only other atmosphere of importance is the pathos which surrounds Sophie and a few other unfortunates. Any feelings of joy are distinctly absent in the novel.

Theme

Theme and satire are very closely interwoven in *The Chrysalids*. Because the themes are generally critical ones, the author tries to make them effective by using satire.

Many of the critical ideas in the novel are pointed directly at the shortcomings of David's society and, indirectly, at our society. The people of Waknuk, for example, purge from their midst anything that is not normal or, at least, does not look like their concept of normal. Mankind has always reacted to things that are distinct from the normal pattern. In primitive societies, deviates are often killed at birth—but sometimes they are worshipped. In our society, we have institutions and clinics to educate and administer to the abnormal; yet there are "freak" shows in every large midway. David's society, despite its concern for the True Image, allows the great-horses to be bred and used. These horses are huge, far bigger than any normal horse. But, they do twice the work of a normal horse at less than twice the feed. For the sake of profit the True Image can be ignored. Hypocrisy, it seems, is a human characteristic, and the people of Waknuk are no different from us.

Another of the author's statements, or themes, is directed specifically at us. This one is less satirical than it is bitter. The graphic description of the Badlands, the deviations, the age of barbarism, the horror of Tribulation, all point out the inherent dangers of nuclear war and, perhaps more effectively, the finality of such a war.

But the chief critical theme is the one implied by the title of the novel. Chrysalid is a term taken from biology. It describes the state through which a larva must pass before becoming an insect. In this state, the larva is wrapped in a hard case or shell, takes no food and is totally inactive. This is precisely the state that Joseph Strorm and his kind are trying to force on humanity. To do this is to deny evolution on one hand, and man's inherent dynamism on the other. The movement is an anti-intellectual one that tries to eliminate both logic and imagination. All this is done in the name of God who, in this case, is used as an excuse, a shield to hide behind for purposes of persecution.

Wyndham's attack on this kind of thing varies from satire to outright bitterness. The satire is directed chiefly at Joseph

Strorm. Since he personifies all that is wrong with the community's religious ideas, he is made to appear as a frustrated buffoon, but a dangerous one. He is a combination of child and Satan, eagerly peeking through keyholes, but with the purpose of destruction in mind.

More often, though, the criticism takes a crueler form, such as Sophie's fate, or Aunt Harriet's. Their stories introduce a sense of helpless frustration for they point out not only the foolishness of the Waknuk philosophy but, also, the futility of trying to defeat it.

Uncle Axel supplies the most apt analysis of the situation, for he tells David that every group of people he sees in his travels thinks that the True Image is themselves. No one, he points out, could ever be sure that the True Image is right, for it comes from *Nicholson's Repentances*, written after Tribulation.

The severity of Wyndham's criticism is tempered only by the Sealanders. Not only do these people offer hope to David and his friends but, by their wish to improve and develop mankind, they give hope to the novel.

Style

This is a novel of plot and theme. The author is concerned with the sociological and psychological implications of a society faced with the after-effects of a nuclear holocaust; therefore, his aims are in the direction of a general impression, rather than the probing of an individual's character, when faced by a certain set of circumstances.

Although considerable opportunity occurs for long descriptive passages, the author does not utilize this. To develop a gruesome description of various forms of deviation would be sensationalizing, and the author has a serious purpose.

Only the character of David is revealed to any extent, and he is the only one who develops appreciably. Sophie is another possible exception. The other characters are one-sided, representative characters like Jacob, or almost caricatures like Joseph Strorm. Most of the characters of the novel seem to fall into groups. The Waknuk group is held together by its religion, the Fringes people by their deviations, and David and his group by their telepathic ability.

The story is told in the first person. This narrative method has advantages for the novel. It is a more personal account and David is more likely to win the reader to his side, against the horrors of Waknuk. Although the method necessitates a limited viewpoint, it is, therefore, a better one for moulding the reader's impressions. The reader is taken into David's confidence and asked to share the secret of his deviation. Above all, there is an air of truth to what David is saying, and this fact intensifies every situation in the novel.

Background in a novel of this type is often very involved. Science fiction by its very nature deals with situations apart from the reader's experience and, therefore, requires long explanations. The peculiarities of David's civilization are related partly by David himself as he explains them to Sophie, but for David to do all of the narration would be tiresome, indeed. Besides, he is a young boy and not likely to know all the information. Conveniently, Uncle Axel explains it to him. Because Axel is a broad-minded, thinking person, the reader is given a fuller, less prejudiced account than he might have received from someone like Joseph Strorm.

It is through mouthpieces like Axel that Wyndham establishes many of his themes. Axel and the Sealand woman deal at great length with the shortcomings of Waknuk's religion. The "other side" is supplied by Joseph, Old Jacob, and David's own reflections. It is interesting that David's childlike questions are asked with a naïvete that makes his elders look ridiculous.

Parallel situations are frequently used for emphasis in the novel. Petra and Aunt Harriet's unfortunate baby are born at the same time (and in the same chapter). Old Jacob's rumbling about the need for a scapegoat is juxtaposed with the discovery of Petra's powers. This kind of juxtaposition is a tool the author uses to point out the dangers of living in Waknuk.

Irony, too, is a frequent device in *The Chrysalids*, but this seems natural in view of David's peculiar ability. Because of their telepathic ability, David and his friends usually have an extra view of matters, and this creates irony. Petra, for example, is given a certificate of normalcy but, by Waknuk's standards, she is more of a deviate than Sophie. David and the others and, also, the reader, are aware of this.

Deus ex machina is a device that was frequently employed in ancient Greek plays. In these classical dramas, a god would descend to the scene of the action and resolve all the difficulties. Although this seems dramatically weak to modern audiences, it is a simple and neat way to end a play. Wyndham has been accused of using a similar device with the Sealand people. They seem to have nothing to do with the novel and appear, almost miraculously and very conveniently, at the end of the novel to rescue David and the others just when the situation is most dramatically hopeless.

In the defence of the author, though, it must be pointed out that Uncle Axel quite clearly establishes the existence of societies outside Labrador. Sealand, like Labrador, escapes the worst of Tribulation and the Sealand people, who had never come to Labrador before, come this time only because of Petra's phenomenal powers.

The story is given unity and coherence chiefly through the fact that it deals with the events surrounding one character; but, the use of dreams is a further means. Coherence is maintained, too, by the developing series of incidents that lead to David's eventual discovery and flight.

Review Questions

1. Describe "blasphemy" and "offence." How are each of these treated?

2. Who are the Fringes people? How does their existence come about?

3. Why is David's home life a rather uninviting one?

4. Who are the Old People? What evidence is there of a civilization they had?

5. What is Uncle Axel's purpose in the novel?

6. What does the crisis with Sophie and Alan Ervin do for the story?

7. In what way is Petra an example of irony in the novel?

8. Describe Aunt Harriet's contribution to the novel.

9. What is Old Jacob symbolic of?

10. Why is Anne's marriage such a crisis?

11. In what way is David's flight to the Fringes inevitable? What finally brings it about?

12. Who are the Sealand people? How are they brought into the story?

13. Who is the Spider-Man? What is his part in the story?

14. Describe the final fate of Sophie.

15. What happens to all the protagonists at the end of the story?

Suggested Study Topics

1. One of the emotions that good science fiction should arouse is discomfort. Does *The Chrysalids* do this?
2. The Sealand lady says, "But ours is a superior variant . . . and where may that not take us some day?" Discuss the possibilities open to a race that can communicate the way they do.
3. What are some of the advantages and disadvantages that are part of being telepathic?
4. Justify Joseph Strorm's position, and the position of those in Waknuk who believe in their religion.
5. Explain the flaws in Joseph Strorm's arguments.
6. Describe and evaluate the philosophy of the Fringes people.
7. Are there any possibilities of disillusion for David and his friends in the Sealand society.
8. Is this book in any sense irreverent? At what, exactly, is the criticism directed?
9. What examples in history do we have of the type of persecution in Waknuk?
10. Discuss several reasons for the author's choice of Labrador as the general setting of the novel.
11. Is the novel one of hope or despair?
12. Discuss the methods by which the author achieves such a high degree of credibility in the novel.
13. Weakness in character seems to be a prominent element in *The Chrysalids*. Discuss.
14. What elements of Waknuk society exist in ours?
15. Would this novel make a successful movie? Explain your answer.
16. Discuss the significance of the following to the novel's character development, plot and theme:
    a) The episode of Aunt Harriet
    b) The dreams of David
    c) The reappearance of Sophie
    d) The suicide of Anne

THE DAY OF THE TRIFFIDS

Introduction

John Wyndham's ideas for *The Day of the Triffids* were adapted from many sources, since he was a regular reader of science fiction. Also, for several years before this novel appeared (1951), Wyndham, himself, had written science fiction short stories for the popular American magazines, *Amazing Stories* and *Wonder Stories*.

In *The Day of the Triffids*, Wyndham joins two ideas from his files, one on the theme of universal blindness and the other on the theme of a plant menace. Other stories that may have influenced his handling of the two major plot situations in *The Day of the Triffids* are *Seeds from Space*, by Laurence Manning (*Wonder Stories*, June, 1930), with its intelligent plants grown from unknown seeds, and Edgar Wallace's short story, *The Black Grippe* from the March, 1920 issue of *Strand Magazine*, in which the entire world is stricken blind for six days.

Parallels have also been drawn between this novel by Wyndham and *The Time Machine* and *War of the Worlds* by an earlier British science fiction writer, H.G. Wells. Wells and Wyndham both succeed in combining invention with a powerful interest in the effects on human society of their inventions. For both novelists, the main interest lies not in the invention itself (which acts as a device, whether it is a time machine, blindness or triffids), but in a detailed examination of human morality. It is this social and moral concern, along with a talent for engaging the reader's interest from the very first page, that has contributed to the early and continuing success of *The Day of the Triffids*.

The Day of the Triffids earned John Wyndham an international reputation as a skilled science fiction writer. This success attracted the attention of the American movie industry and, in 1963, Allied Artists released *The Day of the Triffids* as a film. A reasonably faithful copy of the novel, the film frightened audiences around the world.

Wyndham's novel has become a classic example of British science fiction, and has been translated into a number of other languages. It is now studied in both high schools and universities all over the world.

Plot Summary

The Day of the Triffids is a chilling tale of the future. A spectacular explosion of comets in space causes mass blindness on earth. At the same time an agricultural experiment goes awry and hordes of giant plants emerge, threatening the existence of mankind. These plants are called triffids, a name which describes their most prominent feature, a three-pronged root.

Bill Masen, the narrator and central character in *The Day of the Triffids*, is the only child of parents who live in a southern suburb of London. His father works for the inland revenue department, and hopes that his son will become an accountant. However, Bill shows no aptitude for figures and, in this regard, is a source of disappointment to his father.

Bill's early acquaintance with triffids is a deciding influence in his choice of a career. While still a boy, he is stung by a triffid growing in his own garden, thus achieving at an early age the dubious distinction of being one of the first people in England to experience a triffid attack. This "uncomfortable distinction" stimulates his interest in the triffids, so that when he leaves school he begins work with the Arctic & European Oil Company which, before the recognition of the economic importance of triffids, had been the Arctic & European Fish Oil Company. Bill's work is concerned with the production side of the company's business, and leads to his friendship with Walter Lucknor, who becomes something of an expert on triffids. While working with triffids, Bill suffers the sting which forces him to spend time in hospital before the fateful day of May 8. Thus, he is one of the few people to escape the blindness caused by the collision of comets.

When he leaves the hospital that morning, Bill heads for central London, where he meets Josella, whom he rescues from the clutches of a blind man. At the university, Bill and Josella join Beadley's party. However, both of them are captured by Coker's party of blind men and women and, so, are unable to leave London with Beadley's group. The mysterious fatal disease which struck the people suddenly results in Josella's escape to the Sussex Downs. She is separated from Bill, who is travelling with Coker to Wiltshire in search of both Beadley and Josella. In Wiltshire, Bill finds only Miss Durrant and her party who, originally, were part of Beadley's people; they have gone elsewhere. After further searching, Bill heads for the Sussex Downs, where he is reunited with Josella, at Shirning Farm. After some years, Bill, leading a group of people at the farm, escapes to the Isle of Wight where Beadley and his people have established safe residence. From the Isle of Wight, Bill writes the account of his experiences which is *The Day of the Triffids*.

The chaos that follows the mass blindness and the emergence of the triffids draws much of its horror from the fact that no one, including Bill Masen, fully understands what is happening as civilization collapses and gives way to a nightmare of pain and horror.

Characters in the Novel

BILL MASEN: The narrator and central character of the novel; shows himself to be both sensible and practical; his struggle to adjust to the chaos of his new world provides the main conflict in the story.

JOSELLA PLAYTON: A conventional woman, twenty-four years old; accompanies Bill Masen; shows strength of character when she takes charge at Shirning Farm.

THE LANDLORD OF THE ALAMEIN ARMS: Minor character; through his pathetic suicide, acquaints the reader with the tragedy that the mass blindness has brought to society.

BILL'S FATHER: Minor character; offers contrast to his son, in his aptitude for accounting; killed before the action of the novel begins.

UMBERTO CHRISTOFORO PALANGUEZ: Pilot of Latin descent; might have been the person responsible for spreading the triffid seeds around the world.

WALTER LUCKNOR: One of Bill's colleagues at the Aretic & European Oil Company.

WILFRED COKER: First appears in front of the university; devises the scheme to kidnap sighted people to lead groups of the blind; causes the separation of Bill from Josella's and Beadley's party.

THE COLONEL: In charge of the organization of Beadley's group.

MICHAEL BEADLEY: Explains the dimensions of the tragedy to his group; successfully establishes a community on the Isle of Wight.

SANDRA TELMONT: Executive secretary to Beadley's group.

ELSPETH CARY: Records events for Beadley's community.

IVAN SIMPSON: A pilot for Beadley; he is the means by which Wyndham informs Bill of Beadley's adventures and Coker's experiences.

MISS BERR: A nurse

DR. E.Y. VORLESS, D.Sc.: A professor of sociology at the University of Kingston; emphasizes the need to adapt to a new way of life.

ALF: A blind man at the university.

MISS DURRANT: A young woman who opposes Dr. Vorless at the conference of Beadley's group; her views prove to be mistaken.

THE YOUNG MAN WITH THE PISTOL: Shoots one of Bill's captors; helps to underline the growing violence in the city.

THE YOUNG GIRL WHO COMMITS SUICIDE: One of the blind people for whom Bill is responsible; she adds to the pathos in the novel by committing suicide.

STEPHEN BRENNELL: A young man who stops Bill and Coker in the village of Beaminster, with a rifle; later becomes friendly and helps in the search for Beadley.

SUSAN: Nine or ten years old; only survivor of her village; first to notice the light from Shirning Farm; helps to reunite Josella and Bill.

DENNIS AND MARY BRENT: They own Shirning Farm; blind but seek to help Bill and Josella.

JOYCE TAYLOR: A woman on the Shirning Farm.

MR. TORRENCE: A military commander who tries to impose martial law on the community to contain the chaos; this threat, posed by Torrence, hastens the flight of the Shirning group to the Isle of Wight.

Critical Analysis

CHAPTER 1

The End Begins

William Masen—the name of the narrator, as revealed in the second chapter—felt there was something wrong from the moment he woke up. It was eight o'clock on a Wednesday morning, but the day seemed to have the silence of a Sunday.

He learned later that he owed his unusual survival to the "sheer accident" of being in hospital, with his head "wreathed in bandages," at the crucial time. However, when he awoke that Wednesday morning, he felt only annoyance at the lack of sounds around him for, usually, someone came to wash and tidy him up at precisely three minutes past seven. In addition, he was beginning to feel hungry. Finally, that day—Wednesday, May 8—was especially important to him, because the bandages covering his eyes were due to be removed.

The day outside, with its unusual silence, was becoming more and more alarming. Though the hospital was situated at a busy intersection, on this day there was no noise of traffic. There was not even the sound of birds. The only sounds from the street were five sets of shuffling footsteps, three distant voices, the hysterical sobs of a woman and the humming of wires in the wind. He began to feel fear.

Bill was tempted to peep from under his bandages. However, having been blind for over a week, he resisted the impulse for fear of the effect sudden light might have upon his eyes. He pushed the call bell, but there was no response. Finally, he stumbled to the door, reached the corridor and shouted for his breakfast. The reply was frightening. Many different sounds, made up of seemingly hundreds of abnormal voices, responded. Hurriedly, he closed the door and returned to bed; his fear increased by a terrifying scream from the street below. Though he was tempted once more to remove his bandages, he did not do so, lacking the courage to face the possibility of blindness.

Lying in bed, he was convinced that today was Wednesday, because of the remarkable happenings of the previous day. The day before, the earth, it had been reported, had passed through a cloud of comet debris. As a result, the sky had been filled with brilliant green flashes that had astonished everyone and had kept radio commentators busy. The last thing Bill had heard before drifting off to sleep was the radio report that the flashes were disappearing and that the earth would be out of the debris area in a few hours.

At last, he decided to risk removing the bandages. This he did cautiously. With relief, he found that he could see. However, he spent a full hour accustoming himself to the light in the room. Then, carefully putting on a pair of dark glasses, he looked from the window. He saw only one or two people, who seemed to be wandering about in a strange, aimless fashion. He also observed that not a single chimney in sight was emitting smoke.

Bill took his clothes from the closet and dressed. His earlier panic now seemed strange to him, and he was sure that somewhere in the hospital someone must have the situation under control.

He left his room and opened the door to a surgical ward containing about twenty bedridden patients. One of the patients, grumbling at the lack of light, asked Bill to open the curtains. He did so, but the same man repeated his request. Bill fled from the room.

Bill felt shaky again. It was hard to believe that all of the men he had just seen could be blind, and yet the evidence was clear.

In another ward, he found two men lying dead on the floor. On the stairs, he almost tripped over another dead man.

The most frightening scene was in the main hall, where a tightly packed mob of patients in nightclothes milled around helplessly, unable to find the doorway. It looked like a picture of hell, as people were killed and injured in the confusion. Bill retreated to his room once more. After a while, he found a service staircase that led him out to the yard.

In the midst of his nightmare, he felt the desperate need for a drink. He entered a nearby pub, which was deserted, except for the landlord, a "large-bellied, red-faced man," who was throwing bottles of gin aside in his search for other liquor. The man was blind, and told Bill that everyone was probably blind because of the effect of the comet. The landlord's wife, despairing at her blindness and the blindness of her children, had killed both herself and them. Bill left the drunken man as he proceeded unsteadily upstairs to commit suicide.

CHAPTER 2

The Coming of the Triffids

Bill set down his personal record of the events that had led to the tragedy that had overcome the world.

His family was indistinguishable from millions of others. His father worked for the inland revenue department, and they lived in a southern suburb of London. Bill's lack of skill in mathematics was a disappointment to his father and, until Bill was thirteen or fourteen years of age, he did not know what career he wanted. The triffids decided the matter. They provided Bill with a job and, also, indirectly saved Bill's life since a triffid sting landed him in hospital during the "comet debris."

Since Bill worked with triffids, he knew that most of the speculation about them was nonsense. They were not spontaneously generated; they were not mystical messengers of coming disaster; and their seeds were not some strange form of life from space. Their appearance, Bill was convinced, was the result of "a series of ingenious biological meddlings" and probably accidental. Information about them had been scarce for two reasons: there were no records kept in the region in which they evolved, and the current political conditions had lead to a feeling of peace.

Five-sixths of the world of Bill's youth was peaceful. Travel was unhindered, weapons were unnecessary and more of the earth was gradually being won for agriculture. However, a couple of bad harvests made the people aware of the growing population problem. But, the crisis was postponed by the satellites which every major country had circling the earth. They were fearsome weapons since some of them were rumored to contain materials for chemical warfare.

The situation remained relatively stable until the appearance of Umberto Christoforo Palanguez, a pilot who presented the Arctic & European Fish Oil Company with what was later realized to be the first specimen of triffid oil. Alarmed at the effect this potent oil would have on their trade, the company officials promised the pilot an enormous sum of money to fly a quantity of triffid seeds out of Russia. Umberto left on his mission, but never returned. Bill speculated that he had been shot down by Russian planes and that, as a result, the seeds had been released over the earth. Bill could think of no other reason why that plant, intended to be kept secret, should have so suddenly become known almost everywhere.

Bill's introduction to a triffid came early, because his family had one of them in their garden. His father examined the plant carefully, noting the woody trunk from which the stem sprang, the three small, bare sticks beside the stem and the curious, funnel-like formation at the top of the stem. It was about four feet high at the time, and was probably half grown.

The first report of a walking triffid came from Indo-China, though the Russians must have known about the phenomenon earlier. Similar reports of walking plants followed quickly from most places bordering on the equator. When the reports appeared in print, Bill's family realized that their mysterious plant was identical to the triffids, except in size. From newsreels, Bill observed that the plants walked on the three blunt projections from the trunk, sliding the two front "legs" forward and then bringing the rear "leg" up to meet them.

Bill loosened the soil around the trunk of his plant to encourage it to walk. As he crouched over the plant, he seemed to be struck a tremendous blow. He recovered consciousness in bed, and one side of his face was covered with a red welt. He had been one of the first people in England to be struck by a triffid's sting. Only the immaturity of his plant had saved him from death. His father burned the plant.

Now that walking plants were an established fact, publicity about them increased. At last, after a great deal of public debate, a name was coined for them—triffids—which focussed on their three-legged feature. However, interest dragged until other features of the plant became known. First, some disgust was aroused when it was discovered that the plants were carnivorous, and consumed insects which it trapped in the sticky cone at the top of its stem. Later, when it was discovered that the whorl at the top of the stem contained a ten-feet-long stinging weapon with enough poison to kill a man, wholesale destruction of triffids followed. The hysterical assault on the plants began to stop when it was realized that the weapon could be cut off and that it took the plant about two years to replace the dangerous sting. It thus became fashionable to have one or two clipped plants in the garden for amusement.

Control of the plants in temperature zones was no problem. In tropical areas, they were a lurking menace. However, various weapons were developed to slice off the top of the dangerous plants.

Research into the nature, habits and constitution of the triffids followed. For example, it was revealed that the largest specimen ever observed in the tropics measured nearly ten feet. No European specimen over eight feet had been seen, and the average height was a little over seven feet. The triffids also adapted easily to a wide variety of climatic and soil conditions, and appeared to have no natural enemies except man. However, other important features of the triffids received no notice until later. For example, they always aimed their sting at the head, and did so with remarkable accuracy. Second, they always lurked near the bodies of their victims, a characteristic that became meaningful when it was realized that they devoured the dead flesh by using the stinging tendril to "pull shreds from a decomposing body and lift them to the cup of its stem." Finally, there was little interest in the three bare sticks at the base of the stem of the triffids; the rapid tapping of the sticks against the stem was dismissed as "some strange form of triffidian amatory exuberance," or love talk.

The distinction of being one of the first to be stung by a triffid probably stimulated Bill's interest in triffids. Thus, when the Arctic & European Fish Oil Company dropped the word "Fish" from its title and, in common with other companies, began to farm triffids on a large scale, in order to extract valuable oils and juices, he obtained a job with the company. Before his father and mother were killed in a holiday airbus crash five years later, all other competing oils had been driven off the market, and Bill and others who had been in on the project at the beginning were apparently well set for life.

One of Bill's colleagues, Walter Lucknor, though not well qualified agriculturally, commercially or scientifically, came nearer to understanding the triffids than any man. It was he who first implanted the idea in Bill's mind that the tapping of the triffids' bare sticks against the stem was actually a means of communicating with one another. Lucknor had become convinced that the triffids "talked." From this, he concluded that they possessed intelligence of some kind. This was confirmed, he argued, by other behavior of the triffids. They always struck at an unprotected part of the victims, such as the head or the hands. Further, they frequently struck at the eyes, as though knowing that a blind man lost his superiority. In fact, he declared, if it were a choice for survival between a triffid and a blind man, he would choose the triffid, because their needs for survival were far less complex than man's. Thus, he disturbed Bill by speaking of the triffids as competitors.

After a year or two, Bill began to travel abroad more, studying triffid growing methods. Lucknor went into the research department, where he developed his discoveries. He proved, to his own satisfaction at least, that the triffids possessed a well-developed intelligence. He also established the fact that, deprived of their bare sticks, the triffids gradually deteriorated. Further, he discovered that the infertility rate of triffid seeds was almost 95 per cent. This last fact was comforting. For, in late August, when the triffid seed pods burst, the air was full of the white seeds, which had been shot into the air like steam. Lucknor also discovered that the quality of the triffid extracts improved if the plants retained their stings. As a result, the practice of clipping was discontinued, and workers wore protective devices.

Bill was working with Lucknor when the accident which landed him in hospital occurred. Though he was wearing a wire mesh mask, a triffid sting lashed so viciously at his face that a few drops of poison entered his eyes. Lucknor's swift administration of antidote saved Bill's sight, but he still had to spend over a week in bed, in the dark. During that time, he decided that, if he had not lost his sight, he would apply for a transfer. He spent hours thinking of other work he could do should the transfer be refused. In the light of events to come, his contemplation was idle.

CHAPTER 3

The Groping City

Bill left the pub and made for London. Though it was a beautiful day, he felt lonely, for there were only a few, groping people to be seen, and there was no traffic.

He was hungry, but though there were untended stores, he could not bring himself simply to take food. His nearly thirty years of civilized existence prevented him from doing that. However, when he came to a store whose window had been smashed by a taxi which had mounted the sidewalk, he collected enough food for a meal and left a fair price for what he took.

He ate his meal in a garden opposite the store. While he relaxed there, he heard a girl's voice singing:

So we'll go no more a-roving
So late into the night,
Though the heart be still as loving,
And the moon be still as bright.

The song ended in the sound of sobbing. Unable to endure any more, Bill left the garden quietly.

He found even Hyde Park Corner, a place where amateur speakers gathered on soap boxes, was almost deserted. There were a few derelict cars and trucks, and a small number of men and women who were feeling their way about.

In Park Lane, Bill encountered a man who had been blind since before the latest calamity. When Bill told him what had happened, the man received the news with a bitter laugh and strode off, "wearing an exaggerated air of independence."

There were more people, now, groping their way and occasionally colliding with one another. One blind young man overtook a woman carrying a small child. When he learned that the child could see, he insisted that it point out what was in the shop windows. The child mentioned apples and figs and, immediately, the young man broke the window that was being described. He reached inside and took out two oranges, one of which he gave to the woman. She hesitated to accept the stolen fruit but, at last, yielded to his insistence that that was the only way she could obtain food.

Piccadilly Circus, a busy intersection in London, seemed more crowded, though there were probably fewer than a hundred people there. They were remarkably quiet and seemed dazed. The one exception was an elderly, thin man who was emphatically warning people against the wrath of God. The sound of his voice was interrupted by the noise of drunken singing, as a file of twenty-five or thirty men appeared, each one holding onto the shoulders of the man ahead. They were led by a sighted man, who promised his comrades more liquor and women. When he grabbed a girl to give to his friends, Bill intervened, but he was knocked unconscious. When he recovered his senses, Bill realized that he had probably been fortunate that nothing worse had happened. In any case, he reflected, the sighted man had at least undertaken to look after his companions, and the women would probably go willingly with the men when hunger became a problem.

At the Regent Palace Hotel, Bill, sipping a brandy and smoking a cigarette, realized that everything he had known before was now finished. His way of life and his plans and ambitions were now wiped out. In a way, he felt fortunate that he had no one dependent on him. Thus, his overwhelming response was a feeling of release. The problems he would have to face would be new ones. He would be his own master, and not "shoved hither and thither by forces and interests" that he "neither understood nor cared about." He finished his brandy and went out to see what his new world had to offer.

CHAPTER 4

Shadows Before

Bill entered Soho, a seedy part of the city, and found that there were more people in the streets. Perhaps hunger had driven them outside. As he watched them struggling in front of broken shop windows, he felt that they were already fast losing "ordinary restraints." Though he felt guilty at being able to see when they could not, he did not help them. He concluded that it was best to avoid them.

A sudden scream stilled the street. In an alley, Bill discovered a burly, blind man who was beating a sighted girl he had fastened to his wrist with a rope. Bill rescued her.

Bill took the girl to a nearby pub, which was empty. She was, he observed, about twenty-four years of age, and wore clothes of good quality. Recovered from her ordeal, she confessed to feeling shame at her handling of catastrophe. She was, she declared, usually self-reliant but, thinking that she was the only sighted person left, she had panicked. She told her story to Bill. Her name was Josella Playton and, on the Monday evening preceding the tragedy, she had attended a party. On the Tuesday evening, struggling to recover from a hangover, she had taken a sleeping pill. On the fateful Wednesday morning, her father had awakened her with the news that he was blind. To her horror, she had found that the servants were also blind. She had taken out her car to find the doctor, but it had run out of gasoline halfway down Regent Street. At that point, she had been captured by the blind man from whom Bill had rescued her.

As they talked, Bill's sense of release was spoiled by a realization of the grimness which lay ahead. The future, he speculated, might involve either a lonely existence, or else the gathering together of a selected group of people to provide leadership. His thoughts were interrupted by Josella, who declared that she had better return to her father, since it was now after four o'clock.

Outside, Bill stopped at a shop to pick up two sheath knives. Then Josella and Bill drove in an abandoned car to her home. In the driveway, they came upon the body of Pearson, the gardener. As Josella crouched over him, a triffid attacked. Bill managed to mangle its stem with his bare hands. He was stung but unhurt, because the triffid's poison supply was almost exhausted. On a path around the house, they found the body of

Annie, one of the servants. When they looked into the lounge hall, they saw a triffid standing in the middle of the room. Beside it was the body of Josella's father. As they watched, another triffid approached them, and they retreated quickly to the car. Bill recalled Lucknor's declaration that triffids were in a better position to survive than blind men. When another triffid approached, Josella panicked. It seemed almost to be listening as it paused by the gatepost. Then, with a clatter of its bare stalks, it lumbered away.

Bill started the car and made off toward London once more.

CHAPTER 5

A Light in the Night

Bill drove toward Clerkenwell, where there was a place that made the best triffid guns and masks in the world. On the way, Josella and Bill were horrified to observe a crowd of panic-stricken people who seemed to be pursued by a triffid. Near King's Cross Station, their car was stopped and beseiged by a mob. Bill and Josella escaped and resumed their journey in a station wagon.

At Clerkenwell they obtained several excellent triffid guns, thousands of little steel boomerangs for the guns, and some wire mesh helmets. Bill then decided that they had better find an apartment to serve as their base and, afterward, go in search of clothes and dinner.

They found a luxuriously furnished apartment with ease, and Josella left to obtain clothes. When Bill left on the same mission, he witnessed the tragic sight of a blinded young couple who committed suicide by leaping from an apartment balcony.

Two hours later, Bill prepared a meal on a kerosene stove while Josella dressed in some of her new clothes. As he waited for her, he looked reflectively from the window, saying good-by to the world he had known, for he was sure that all that it faced was "the long, slow, inevitable course of decay and collapse." When Josella appeared, she was dressed elegantly, a gesture that was also her farewell to the old world.

At dinner, Josella told Bill more of her life story. She had almost married at nineteen. When her family objected, she had moved out on her own. During that period, she had written a best-selling book, *Sex Is My Adventure*. It had not, she explained, been a wicked book, but it had created a sensation, as Bill remembered. Following this success, she had returned home.

As they relaxed together, they discussed the future. Bill observed that they must leave the towns and cities because of the health problems posed by the number of corpses. Josella informed him that she knew of a lovely old farmhouse on the north side of the Sussex Downs. It was on the side of the hills, had a supply of water and also had facilities for generating electricity. They postponed a decision about their final destination, and discussed acquiring a truck for their supplies.

Drawing up a list of their needs took them till midnight. They then retired for the night.

In the night, Josella wakened Bill to inform him that she had observed a light outside. From the window, Bill saw that, toward the northeast, there was a bright beam like that of a searchlight. It seemed to indicate the presence of someone else who could see. They decided to investigate it in the morning.

CHAPTER 6

Rendezvous

The next morning, Bill and Josella made their way toward the university tower, the source, they had decided, of the signal light. Once there, they discovered a crowd of blind people milling in front of the gates. They were led by a sighted man, who was trying to persuade those inside the grounds to help the blind. When they refused, he attempted to climb the gates. However, the crowd was driven off by a burst of machine-gun fire. Bill understood the tragedy of the situation clearly, as those inside the grounds obviously did: either the sighted could devote themselves to saving what they could from the catastrophe, or else they could devote themselves to stretching out the lives of the blind a little longer.

Bill and Josella climbed the wall surrounding the university tower and were taken to see a man known as the colonel. A precise man who valued efficiency, he made a note of their names and addresses and then sent them to see Michael Beadley, who introduced them to the group's executive secretary, Sandra Telmont. Beadley explained that there were about thirty-five people in their group, twenty-eight of them sighted. They intended to leave London the next day, after gathering the supplies they needed. He was surprised to learn that Bill had a station wagon packed with anti-triffid gear, thinking such equipment relatively unimportant. He sent Bill and Josella to exchange the station wagon for a truck, unloaded the wagon, and obtained a list of food supplies. Before Bill left, Beadley supplied him with a pistol.

On their first trip out, Bill and Josella were able to obtain two trucks, which they brought back to the university tower filled with canned goods and household supplies. They returned from their second expedition with two more trucks. When Beadley inspected their contribution, he looked with disapproval on the cases containing Bill's anti-triffid gear. Beadley reluctantly agreed to allow the equipment to be transported with the other supplies. He obviously seemed to regard Bill as being "a bit unsound on the subject of triffids." This lack of concern over the triffids worried Bill and Josella.

Bill and Josella went out into a garden in Russell Square to practise with their triffid guns. While there, they were photographed by Elspeth Cary, "the official record" of the group. The three discussed the triffid problem, and Miss Carey seemed more inclined than Beadley had been to take them seriously. When Ivan arrived in a helicopter, she left to take his picture as he landed.

Left alone, Bill and Josella talked. Josella expressed her shock at how easily people had lost a world that had seemed so safe and certain. Bill agreed. It was the very simplicity of the catastrophe which made it so shocking. Familiarity made one forget the complex balance of things which made a secure world. Thus, without sight, all of man's power and the miracles he had wrought were nothing. As they chatted, Josella observed that she did not think she was going to like the new, strange world. Her observation seemed odd to Bill. He preferred to find out first what the world was going to be like, and then to do something about what he disliked. However, he did not say anything about his opinion.

Bill and Josella returned to the university tower for a meeting of the group.

CHAPTER 7

Conference

To their surprise, Bill and Josella found almost a hundred people gathered for the meeting. There were more young women by a ratio of four to one and, as Josella pointed out, most of them could not see. However, most of the blind women had been so since before the present calamity and had been included in the group for their skill in coping with their disability.

Michael Beadley addressed the meeting first. He stressed the need for a positive attitude. Mankind, he explained, had faced disaster before. In the present situation, the survivors had "the means, the health, and the strength" to build a new society. His speech seemed to reassure the group.

The colonel spoke next. He informed the people that they would be leaving the city at 1200 hours the next day. All their basic requirements had now been collected, with a view to making the group self-sufficient for a minimum of one year. Their destination would be a country boarding school or a large country mansion. The colonel's practical manner had a further reassuring effect.

Miss Berr, a nurse with excellent nursing qualifications, spoke next. She informed the people that she would inoculate them against a variety of things before they left the hall.

The final speaker was Dr. E.H. Vorless, an elderly professor of sociology from the University of Kingston. His words sparked vigorous debate. The society they had known, he explained, was gone, and with it the old customs, laws and morality. The new situation demanded new ways, and the one basic principle would have to be the survival of the race. Thus, he continued, there would be a simple division of tasks: the men would work and the women would have babies. They would be able to support a limited number of women who could not see, because they would bear sighted babies, but there was no place for men who could not see. One member of the audience, a tall, purposeful-looking woman, asked the professor whether he was suggesting the abolition of the marriage law. He replied that they must make laws suitable for the new situation. However, he insisted, anyone deciding to join the group must abide by the rules of the group. Any others would have to form their own community. A rambling discussion followed.

During the discussion, Bill and Josella went to receive their shots from Nurse Berr. When they returned to their seats, they discussed the reaction of the audience. In view of what had been said, Bill seemed doubtful that many people would want to join the group. Josella took a more practical view. In a choice between having babies and being cared for or adhering to a principle that might mean no babies and no one to look after you, women, she explained, might not be so doubtful. After all, she observed, she was talking about real women, not those of romantic fantasies. All that worried her, she revealed, was how many babies would be expected.

After an hour or so, the meeting broke up. All of those wishing to join the group were to inform Beadley of their decision by ten o'clock the next morning.

Bill and Josella wandered out of doors. Bill told her that he would be proud and happy if she bore his baby. She answered that she would like that, too, but added a practical observation. It was clear to her that the blind girls would have to be looked after and, probably, each man would have to take care of two blind women as well as one sighted woman. Bill was startled by her words. However, she explained her views more extensively. Human beings would have to be much more like a tribe than before. Moreover, those who had survived with their sight owed it to at least a few others to justify the advantage they enjoyed. The choice, she insisted, was obvious. The sighted could give to the few blind persons who came with them the chance of a full life or they could withhold that chance because of the prejudices they had been taught. Bill agreed, grudgingly, and Josella expressed pleasure at his understanding. Mischievously, she added that she would choose two sensible girls for him.

As they sat together, someone in the building played a recording of a Strauss waltz. Bill and Josella danced together, "on the brink of an unknown future, to an echo from a vanished past."

CHAPTER 8

Frustration

Bill awoke suddenly to the clanging of a bell and voices shouting "Fire!" As he went downstairs, he tripped and fell, and lost consciousness.

When he awoke again, he was lying on a bed with his hands tied. A blind man, Alf, entered and explained what had happened. The fire had been a false alarm engineered by Coker, the man who earlier had led the mob at the university gates. In the confusion of the false alarm, Coker's blind colleagues had captured some of the sighted people from the university group. Each sighted man was to be a captive of a small blind party and act as their eyes, until help arrived from outside. However, Alf expressed his opinion that no help would come.

Later, Coker entered and showed Bill the district he had assigned to him. He tried to get news of Josella, but was unsuccessful.

Next morning, handcuffed and chained to two blind men wielding knives, Bill set out by truck on his first search. There were fifty-two people in his party. First, he found them a place to stay, "a glorified boardinghouse." The next couple of days were spent gathering supplies. The work was difficult, because every step demanded Bill's helping presence. However, he decided he would stay until the group was set up properly, and then escape to rejoin Josella.

On the fourth or fifth morning, two of the party were found to be ill. Bill found that they both had high temperatures and complained of agonizing pain in the bowels. He had them moved to an empty house nearby. At noon, the same day, there was another setback. Bill and his party came upon a group of men looting a grocery store. Their leader, a red-haired young man, pulled out a pistol and began shooting. One of the men to whom Bill was chained was killed. Bill overpowered his other captor and removed the handcuffs and chain.

The young man with the pistol began to follow Bill's party, probably with a view to discovering their headquarters. Bill, pretending to be blind, kept him in sight. Suddenly, one of Bill's group doubled up with pain and fell to the ground. The young man had approached him cautiously and then very deliberately shot him in the head. That done, he walked away from the party, a grim look on his face. On returning to the boarding house, Bill discovered that two more men and a woman had become ill.

The next day, while collecting provisions from a store, Bill's party was attacked by triffids. Some of the men were killed, and Bill had great difficulty in leading the rest to safety.

On his return to the boarding house, Bill found that one of the sick men had died and the other was obviously dying; there were, also, four new, sick cases. In despair, Bill began to appreciate Beadley's logic in trying to save only a few people. In the midst of his reflections, he was visited by an eighteen-year-old girl. The group, she explained, did not want him to leave, nor did she. They needed him. She had come to offer herself to Bill, because the party believed that, if he had someone like her, he would not leave. Weeping, Bill ushered her out of the room and instructed her to tell her friends that he would not leave.

The next morning, Bill discovered more cases of sickness. Those who could had left, not believing that Bill would stay with the group. Further, the eighteen-year-old girl was sick. She asked Bill to give her something that would put an end to her life. Bill did so. As he watched her, he was overcome with anger at the futility of death. She had not asked him to take her away with him last night; she had asked him to stay with the group, and he did not even know her name.

CHAPTER 9

Evacuation

Bill left the boarding house and, on his way, collected fire-arms and ammunition. He noted that there seemed to be more triffids in the streets.

When he returned to the university, he found the building deserted. However, chalked on a wall, he found an address: Tynsham Manor, Tynsham, near Devizes, Wilts. This, he gathered, was the destination of Beadley's group. He decided to leave for Devizes, a hundred miles away, the next morning, since dusk was now approaching. His transportation would be the truck outside, which still carried his anti-triffid gear and other supplies.

While he relaxed in the garden in Russell Square, he was surprised at being approached by Coker, who had now decided to leave London. By taking precautions, he had escaped the illness which had stricken the others, and was now prepared to admit that the university group had been right in trying to preserve only a small number of able people. Bill and Coker arranged to travel together the next day.

The next morning, each driving a loaded truck, they headed for Devizes. While they rested outside Staines, Coker surprised Bill by quoting poetry, for it seemed to offer a sharp contrast to the kind of language Coker has used outside the gates of the university tower when Coker's mob had tried to storm the grounds. Coker explained that he made his living by professional speech-making. Educated at evening classes, he had found he had a facility with the spoken word, so that he could communicate with any group he faced. On the night of the world catastrophe, he had been addressing a protest meeting, when the police had arrived. To escape, he had hidden all night in a cellar and, thus, had retained his sight.

At the sight of the open country, which still retained its beauty and peace, Bill felt fresh hope and he found himself singing as he drove. At last, just short of Devizes, they entered the village of Tynsham.

CHAPTER 10

Tynsham

At the gates of Tynsham Manor, Bill and Coker were halted by a young woman wielding a shotgun. When they had identified themselves and she had inspected the trucks, she allowed them to proceed to the manor. There, in the huge kitchen of the large, rambling house, they found fifty or sixty people gathered for a meal. There were more men than there had been in Beadley's group, but they were all blind. Of the women, only about half a dozen could see. Very few of the people had belonged to Beadley's party. At the end of the meal, a blind clergyman arose and led the group in prayer.

The leader of the manor party, Bill learned, was Miss Durrant, the woman who had spoken in opposition to Dr. Vorless at the meeting of the university group. Her society, she said emphatically, was to live by Christian standards. They had, she explained, split from Beadley's party, who had gone elsewhere. Her attitude was not warm for, as Coker observed, she wanted help badly but would not admit her need.

In the dining hall, Bill spoke to a young girl who was trying to do some mending by candlelight. As they spoke, the electric lights in the room suddenly went on. Coker had started the generator, which no one else at the manor knew anything about. The girl took exception to Coker's scornful insistence on the importance of practical matters, and told him that he sounded as though he would find Beadley's party more congenial. When the girl left, angrily, Bill echoed her thought that Coker would probably be more at home with Beadley.

CHAPTER 11

And Farther On

Bill spent a wretched, restless night, worrying over Josella. He had not previously realized how much he had counted on finding her at Tynsham. Without her, he felt without direction, for he had assumed that, being freed from Coker's former colleagues, she would have made her way back to the university building and so found the Tynsham address. Now, he did not even know whether she had succumbed to the fatal disease. He decided to remain at the manor for a day or two, making inquiries about Josella, before joining Beadley's group. He did not know what he would do if she were not with Beadley.

Bill's first inquiries proved fruitless. He was not cheered by Coker's observations concerning the manor community. Coker had had a difference of opinion with Miss Durrant. He had argued firmly that the blind men had to be given useful work to take the burden off the shoulders of the sighted; that, in spite of the minister's prayers, the community could not afford to receive any more blind refugees, and that practical measures had to be taken for the future. He felt that the community was already breaking down and could not survive for long. He declared his intention of joining Beadley.

When Miss Durrant told Bill, reluctantly, that Beadley and his party had said they were going somewhere near Beaminster in Dorset, Bill and Coker set off to join them, travelling as before in their two trucks. When they reached the silent village of Steeple Honey, they saw a blind man waving a white cloth from a window. However, as soon as the man came to the door to meet them, a triffid struck and killed him. Bill swiftly killed the attacker, but both Coker and he were shaken by the incident. Clearly, the triffid seemed to have been waiting for the man to appear. Over a drink, Bill explained Walter Lucknor's theories about triffids to Coker. Before they re-entered their trucks, Bill killed two more triffids, that seemed to have arrived to investigate the fate of the first triffid.

They reached Beaminster at about half-past four that same afternoon, but there was nothing to suggest the presence of Beadley. As they drove down the main street, however, a man suddenly emerged from behind two parked trucks and fired a warning shot at them.

CHAPTER 12

Dead End

Bill stopped his truck and got out, while the large, fair-haired man kept the rifle pointed at him. The man was quickly joined by a dark young man and a good-looking girl. They relaxed visibly on finding only two in the newcomers' party, and retired from the street to eat and drink.

The large man was Stephen Brennell, a member of the stock exchange. The girl was a former model who seemed unconcerned about the tragedy, confident that the Americans would arrive to rescue them. The dark young man was merely annoyed at the interruption in his desire to become wealthy by operating a radio store. None of them knew anything of Beadley.

They agreed to let Bill and Coker join them. They all proceeded to Charcott Old House, which Brennell had begun to fortify against anticipated raiding parties from the cities. He seemed disappointed to learn that there was no danger from the cities. Bill noticed flame throwers among their equipment, and remarked that they would be good weapons against triffids. Brennell mentioned that they had already used the flame throwers for that purpose.

That night they all went up on the roof of the house to look for any sign of Beadley's party, thinking that they would probably still continue to employ a signal light at night. There was no signal. Therefore, they divided the surrounding district into areas and went off, the next morning, to make a detailed search.

It was a depressing day for Bill. The condition of the blinded and dead farm animals filled him with disgust for the triffids, who watched carefully over the decay of their victims and seemed able to profit from the disaster that had come to the world. When the party came together again at the end of the day, no one had any news of Beadley. The radio enthusiast had, however, discovered another sighted young man whom he brought to join them. It was the radio man who, that evening, suggested that they continue their search from the air. There were three airfields nearby, and he would obtain a helicopter. He was sure that he could quickly get the knack of flying it.

They flew the helicopter for four days and discovered ten other little groups of people, most of whom seemed to be irrationally confident that the Americans would arrive to rescue them. There was no trace of Beadley's group. The others decided to abandon the search, though that was not Bill's decision. He wanted to find Beadley's party in the hope that Josella was with them.

Once the decision to abandon the search had been taken, Coker addressed the group. The present time, he explained, was only a welcome pause during which the world had adequate supplies of food and equipment. The future was the real problem for, in time, food supplies would go bad and equipment would wear out. People would have to learn to farm the land and to make the materials they needed. Therefore, in his opinion, Miss Durrant's group offered the best chance for the future. They needed help, but they had a good farm and a reasonably self-contained location. He suggested that they should all go to Tynsham. The party agreed.

In the early hours of the following morning, Bill decided that he was not going to accompany them. He wanted to find Josella. When he suddenly remembered her mention of a farmhouse in the Sussex Downs, he knew what he must do. That morning, he climbed into the familiar truck once more, made his farewells, and set off to find Josella.

CHAPTER 13

Journey in Hope

All morning, Bill drove in drenching rain. However, at one o'clock the sun appeared, and his greatest obstacle was his sense of loneliness. All that kept him going was the hope of companionship at the end of the journey.

He had a moment of hopefulness when a helicopter flew overhead, but overhanging trees hid his truck from the pilot, and the craft flew away. Nevertheless, the sight of the helicopter gave him some moral support.

In a village a few miles further on, Bill's truck was stopped by a little girl, nine or ten years of age. She asked Bill to come and see what had happened to her little brother, Tommy. Bill found the boy, about four years of age, dead; he had been killed by a triffid. The girls' parents had been blinded by triffids and later killed, leaving the children alone. The girl, Susan, had been looking after her brother, teaching him to beware of triffids. However, Tommy had been killed when he went out to play. Bill buried the boy and took Susan with him.

The next day, they reached the downs. They searched the hills carefully for any sign of Josella's farmhouse, but without success. The return of the rain hampered their search. That evening, Bill obtained a headlamp from a Rolls Royce and attached the light to the truck. With this "minor searchlight," he pierced the wet darkness, looking for an answering beam of light. At last, a pinpoint of light began to blink out a signal in Morse code. After slow, difficult driving, Bill reached the farmhouse, where he was reunited with Josella.

CHAPTER 14

Shirning

Bill came to Shirning Farm with the intention of taking Josella immediately to join Miss Durrant's group, but things did not work out that way.

First, though the idea of joining a larger group was obviously better, Shirning Farm was charming. Over the past twenty-five years, it had been modernized, so that it was now neat and attractive. Moreover, it had its own well and its own power plant.

In the second place, there were three other people, all blind, with Josella. The lone man, Dennis Brent, was the owner. His wife, Mary, was pregnant. The third person, Joyce Taylor, was recuperating from the poison of a triffid sting. On the fateful night of the world calamity, there had been five people at the farm: the Brents, Joyce Taylor, and another couple, the Dantons. When they awoke the next morning, all of them were blind. Ted Danton had gone to obtain help and had never returned. His wife, Joan, had gone to look for him and had never come back. When a triffid struck Joyce, their danger became apparent to the survivors. Dennis had fashioned a wire net protective helmet and, with the aid of string, had found his way to the nearby village and back. Thus, they had discovered the extent of their danger. Twice more that week, he had gone to the village for supplies. Each time, the triffids had seemed more numerous. Then, "like a miracle," Josella had arrived. As Bill surveyed his companions, he realized the futility of thinking of immediate removal to Tynsham. Joyce was still weak from the triffid poison, and Mary's baby was due too soon for her to make the journey. Consequently, he spent the next little while searching, obtaining not only food, but gas for the generator, hens that were laying, cows that had calved, medical supplies, and other supplies. He also taught Susan how to shoot a triffid gun, because the area was more infested with triffids than any other he had seen.

Bill also heard Josella's story of her experiences. Like Bill, she had been kidnapped from the university building. Her group had also been killed by disease. Returning to the university, she had searched for Bill. However, catching a glimpse of Coker there, and hearing a rifle shot (which Bill had, ironically, directed at a triffid), she had suspected a trap and not entered.

96

She had driven directly to the farm. Her car had obviously made the sound Bill had heard while talking to Coker in Russell Square.

In a way, the worst affected of the original trio was Dennis. Joyce was still weak, and Mary was preoccupied with her pregnancy, but Dennis was like a caged animal. He desperately sought to conquer his blindness and tried feverishly to learn Braille. He was, therefore, grateful for the opportunity to accompany Bill on his foraging.

Three weeks after Mary gave birth to a baby girl, Bill visited Tynsham. He returned with the news that the community no longer existed. It seemed as though it had been destroyed by the plague. Bill had not entered the buildings because there had been no sign of life. A notice had been pinned to the front door, but only one blank corner of it remained. Josella was overcome by the news and Bill sought to reassure her. He succeeded, and she declared she was ready to accept her lot as a farmer's wife, even though their marriage was not "a very proper, authentic kind of marriage."

CHAPTER 15

World Narrowing

From that time on, Bill kept a journal, recording everything he did. From the journal he saw that, within a week of his return from Tynsham, he had begun the task of erecting a wire fence to keep the triffids out. Actually, there were two fences, a lighter fence within the outer fence, and the plan was to keep one hundred acres free of triffids. Thus, it was a heavy job which took some months.

He also tried to learn how to farm, gaining his knowledge from books. It was, he realized, going to be a difficult task, because in the future he would be unable to obtain chemical fertilizers, imported feedstuffs, or none but the simpler kinds of machinery. In addition, knowledge acquired through books had its limitations. However, he was comforted by the fact that he had plenty of time to learn and that, meanwhile, their supplies were adequate.

Bill let a year pass before he visited London again. It still looked as though it might spring to life, though the vehicles in the streets were beginning to rust. His visit a year after that saw more dramatic change. The buildings were beginning to decay, and growing things were beginning to root in crevices everywhere. On an even later visit, he stood in Piccadilly Circus and found himself unable to visualize the crowds which had thronged there. Josella accompanied him only once, partly to obtain clothes for the baby she was expecting. The visit upset her and she made no further trips to London. At the end of the fourth year, Bill visited London for the last time. When a falling building descended on the road behind his truck, he realized the danger the city now held and he confined his trips to smaller towns. Brighton should have been their largest and most convenient center for supplies, but it was apparently in the charge of another group who had blocked the road to the city and erected a sign saying, "Keep Out!" The sign was backed up by a rifle shot. This experience made Bill consider again Stephen's preparations for defence at Charcott Old House. He, therefore, laid in a supply of machine guns, mortars and flame throwers.

In November of the second year, Josella's first baby was born. They named him David. Bill had some misgivings at the birth of the child, in view of the state of the world, but Josella adored him and seemed, then, to worry less about the future.

It was soon after that that Josella drew Bill's attention more closely to the triffids. There were, she remarked, many more of them, a fact that Bill had not noticed. It was Susan who revealed to Bill that the noises he made in his work attracted them. The plants heard the rifle shots, the tractor engine and the lighting generator, and converged on the farm. They seemed, Dennis observed, to be waiting for something, and he could never forget that they had had the intelligence to attack the farm in the first place when its inhabitants were helpless. In response, Bill rigged a variety of traps, and was able to destroy hundreds of triffids. But they still kept massing at the fence. One morning, they broke through and crowded around the house. They had broken down twenty yards or so of the fence, and only with great difficulty was the group able to force them to retreat by assaulting them with flame throwers. Four months later they broke in again. In defence, Bill charged the fence with electricity. However, this could be done for only a few minutes two or three times a day. Unfortunately, the triffids seemed to learn what the sound of the generator motor meant, but the measure did succeed in keeping them out for over a year. Meanwhile, the party continued to learn more about agriculture, and life settled into a routine.

In their sixth year, Bill took Josella for a drive down the coast. As they looked out over the ocean and a small town, she asked him what he thought of their chances of survival. He answered that their chances were slim. They would be better without the triffids, and what was really needed was a biological method for destroying the plants. He did not, he explained, have the knowledge or the facilities to produce a selective killer on a large scale, but he informed her that he had collected a lot of biochemical books and that he would teach David all he could, in the hope that something might be done in the future. This turned Josella's thoughts to the children, and she wondered whether they ought to invent a myth to help explain to them what had happened. Bill replied that the triffids could not really be blamed on anyone. The real cause of the catastrophe lay with the "tightrope" that the old world had walked. Then he revealed to her his conviction that the blindness had not been caused by a comet. That catastrophe, he maintained, had originated with one of the many man made satellites circling the earth. One of them, spreading its contents in space, must have unleashed the radiation which caused the blindness. The mysterious plague which afflicted survivors, he affirmed, must also have come from a similar source. Josella's response was the declaration that the explanation was less horrible than the thought of nature striking blindly at man. At least, the catastrophe was understandable and their children could be warned of the danger of such mistakes in the future.

Later, on the beach, Bill turned over in his mind their dismal prospects. Every year, they seemed to be more imprisoned at the farm because roads were deteriorating and the country was growing wild. Suddenly, as he talked with Josella, a helicopter appeared in the sky. They waved at it wildly, but the pilot ignored them and continued on his course. The appearance of the aircraft banished their feelings of isolation and renewed their hopes for a better life in the future.

CHAPTER 16

Contact

As Bill and Josella approached the farm, they saw a plume of smoke arising from the house. Fearing what might have happened, they struggled home desperately. The helicopter they had seen had landed at the farm because Susan had set the woodpile alight to attract the craft. The pilot was Ivan Simpson, the man who had flown the helicopter at the university. He had learned of Bill's whereabouts from Coker, who had escaped from Tynsham.

Simpson told the story of Beadley's group. They had not gone to Beaminster, as Miss Durrant had said they would, but northeast, into Oxfordshire. They had found an estate there but, after a year or so, the problem of keeping the triffids at bay with fences had become enormous. Therefore, they moved to the Isle of Wight. The triffid problem had again been considerable, but the party had gradually been able to clear the island. Each year now, they simply scoured the island for signs of wind-blown seeds. Beadley's group now searched for other groups which had survived and took those who were willing to join them. However, many of the surviving groups were hostile. Coker, after leaving Tynsham, had taken a small group to Devonshire, but had begun to despair of keeping the triffids at bay, when his party was rescued. Simpson explained that Beadley's group now had enough leisure to devote their attention to developing a chemical means of killing the triffids, and he invited Bill to join them in the effort. Bill was reluctant to leave Shirning, but he and Josella decided that at the end of the summer they would leave for the Isle of Wight.

CHAPTER 17

Strategic Withdrawal

Returning from an expedition to obtain wood, Bill was astonished to see a strange vehicle parked at the farm. It was something between "a cabin cruiser and an amateur-built caravan." Inside the house, four armed men waited. Their leader, Mr. Torrence, described himself as the Commander for the emergency council for the southeast region of Britain. He had arrived to seize the farm. Seventeen more blind people would be shipped in, and would be looked after by Bill and Josella. Susan would be taken to Brighton and put in charge of a group of blind people when she was old enough. By creating organized, self-sustaining units, Torrence explained, they would be able to take control in Europe and so become the dominant nation. Bill was appalled by Torrence's words but pretended to agree to what had been said.

The Shirning group treated their visitors to a good supper and supplied them with drinks. While they enjoyed their entertainment, Bill quietly packed his vehicle, and poured honey into the tank of Torrence's contraption. Later, while the visitors slept, the Shirning party stole out of the house and crashed through the fence with their vehicle. Torrence's men tried to follow, but Bill's doctoring of their gas tank immobilized their vehicle. When Bill looked back, the triffids had already begun to plunge through the fence and into the farmyard.

And so, Bill's personal story joined up with that of the other survivors. That story could be found in Elspeth Cary's history of the colony. It seemed unlikely that anything would come of Torrence's plan, though every now and then there were reports of another farm being overrun by triffids. Thought must now be given to the task ahead, leading to the day when they would cross the water to the mainland and destroy the triffids, once and for all.

Character Sketches

Bill Masen

Bill Masen is an appropriate hero for the novel because he is, first and foremost, an unexceptional human being. He makes small errors and he freely admits to not being very good at some things, as when he speaks of his father's disappointment in him for not having a head for figures. Also, he experiences feelings of fear in the hospital. In the early stages of the novel, he seems to indulge in an apparent fondness for liquor when situations are difficult. Of course, Bill's unexceptional nature is a deliberate creation by the novelist to contribute to the credibility of the narrator. The reader is able to identify more readily with a character who possesses obvious human weaknesses and feels common human emotions. Nevertheless, there are aspects of Bill Masen which make him an admirable hero.

In the first place, he possesses and reveals an attractive sensitivity of nature. He is not a hero without feelings; he frequently expresses deep and tender emotions. For example, the song of a young girl, heard in the midst of the sombre silence of the stricken city, affects him intensely, so that he can hardly endure it and is "unable to see anything more than mistily for a while." Indeed, Bill is touched so greatly by what he sees in the devastated city that he realizes that, in order to survive, he will have to steel himself against his emotional response and face what happens with more composure:

> "You've got to grow a hide," I told myself. "*Got to.*
> It's either that or stay permanently drunk. Things like
> that must be happening all around. They'll go on
> happening. You can't help it. Suppose you'd given
> them food to keep them alive for another few days?
> What after that? You've got to learn to take it, and
> come to terms with it. There's nothing else but the
> alcoholic funk hole. If you don't fight to live your own
> life in spite of it, there won't be *any* survival . . . Only
> those who can make their minds tough enough to stick
> it are going to get through. . . ."

Of course, Bill is incapable of suppressing his own sensitivity, and it continues to find expression throughout the novel. It is evident with particular vividness in the strong sense of nostalgia that engulfs him whenever he sees the signs that tell of the passing of the old way of life. Thus, as he views London from the apartment window, the moment is full of a sweet sadness:

> I wandered across to the window and looked out. Quite consciously I began saying good-by to it all. The sun was low. Towers, spires, and facades of Portland stone were white or pink against the dimming sky. More fires had broken out here and there. The smoke climbed in big black smudges, sometimes with a lick of flame at the bottom of them. Quite likely, I told myself, I would never in my life again see any of these familiar buildings after to-morrow. There might be a time when one would be able to come back—but not to the same place. Fires and weather would have worked on it; it would be visibly dead and abandoned. But now, at a distance, it could still masquerade as a living city.

This awareness of a vanishing way of life is acute, not only face to face with a dying city, but in smaller experiences, too, as is seen in the following brief moment with Josella:

> She seemed to float across the thick carpet. With her hand on the doorknob she stopped, and turned to regard herself solemnly in a long mirror.
> "Some things were fun," she said, and kissed her hand to her reflection.
> "Good night, you vain, sweet vision," I said.
> She turned with a small smile and then vanished through the door like a mist drifting away.
> I poured out a final drop of the superb brandy, warmed it in my hands, and sipped it.
> "Never—never again now will you see a sight like that," I told myself. . . .

Bill's sensitivity persists throughout the novel, though in time the practical problems to be faced lessen its intensity. For example, in later years, when he sees the full effect that time has had on London, he is able to be more objective and rational in remembering the past. True, when he is alone in the country and thinks of the city, he still recalls the pleasantness of the old life but, when he stands among the crumbling ruins, his recollection stands different: ". . . I seemed to recall only the muddle, the frustration, the unaimed drive, the all-pervading clangor of empty vessels, and I became uncertain how much we had lost. . . ." Nevertheless, the tenderness in his nature remains. Not surprisingly, that tenderness finds its expression in a strong sense of compassion for other people. Bill responds sensitively to the feelings and sorrows of the human beings around him. For example, he feels sympathy for the blind men in the ward at the hospital, as they pitifully ask him to draw the curtains to let the sunlight come into the room. Moments later, his heart is torn at the sight of the milling crowd of blind people in the main hall of the hospital and, unable to bear the sight, he flees from the scene. Later, in Piccadilly Circus, when the line of blind men begins to rough up a young girl, he feels impelled to attempt to rescue the terrified creature. Later still, when faced by Josella's sorrow over the death of her father, he is sensitive to her emotions, even though he does not agree with her desire to bury her father's body:

> She would be better for having her cry out. I lit a cigarette and considered the next move. Naturally she was not going to care for the idea of leaving her father as we had found him. She would wish that he should have a proper burial—and, by the looks of it, that would be a matter of the pair of us digging the grave and effecting the whole business. And before that could even be attempted it would be necessary to fetch the means to deal with the triffids that were already there and keep off any more that might appear. On the whole, I would be in favor of dropping the whole thing—but then it was not my father. . . .

There are, however, some appeals which Bill finds himself unable to resist. When he encounters little Susan, who had been left alone following the death of her brother, Bill is faced with the question whether they would bury Tommy—"like the puppies?" His response is immediate: "In all the overwhelming disaster, that was the only grave I dug—and it was a very small one." Perhaps the most moving example in the novel of the depth of Bill's compassion is that of his experience with the young girl, who is one of Coker's people. Her beauty and her youth arouse feelings of sadness in Bill because she offers herself to him as an inducement to stay with the group. As she makes her offer, his emotions are strong. He thinks of what life should have been like for her:

> I looked at her, standing quite straight, her lips trembling slightly. There should have been suitors clamoring for her lightest smile. She should have been happy and uncaring for a while—then happy in caring. Life should have been enchanting to her, and love very sweet. . . .

Of course, Bill rejects her offer. With tears in his eyes, he tells her to leave him and to tell the others that he will stay with them. Thus, when the girl dies, he is enraged with "the stupidity of death." She has so touched his heart in her pathetic sorrow that he is left with the startling realization that he does not even know her name.

Nevertheless, Bill cannot be dismissed as an impractical sentimentalist. On the contrary, he often shows himself to be both sensible and practical. This aspect of his character is underlined early in the novel. For example, during the first anxious moments of that mysterious May 8, he has, in the beginning, a "nasty, empty feeling" at the strange silence which surrounds him. As a result, he tries to apply his reasoning to the situation. It does not help, of course. The situation at that time defies rational explanation. Nonetheless, the attempt is an indication of his usual behavior. Thus, even after being knocked unconscious by the leader of the blind men in Piccadilly Circus, he sees the reasonableness of what has happened:

> With a bit of sense knocked into me, I became thankful that the affair had not fallen out worse. Had the result been reversed, I could scarcely have escaped making myself responsible for the men he had been leading. After all, and whatever one might feel about his methods, he was the eyes of that party, and they'd be looking to him for food as well as for drink.

Bill's sensible, logical frame of mind has given him a glimpse of a truth that is to become increasingly apparent in the days that follow. The situation is so desperate that determined attention to practical matters is the only way to ensure survival. Sentiment and "schoolboy heroics" will not be sufficient. Thus, his common sense enables him to see, clearly, the nature of the problem which the tragedy poses:

> I felt that I ought to be showing these people where to find food. But should I? If I were to lead them to a food shop still intact, there would be a crowd which would not only sweep the place bare in five minutes but would crush a number of its weaker members in the process. Soon, anyway, all the food in the shops would be gone; then what was to be done with the thousands clamoring for more? One might collect a small party and keep it alive somehow for an uncertain length of time—but who was to be taken and who left? No obviously right course presented itself however I tried to look at it.

As one would expect, Bill's common sense enables him to be practical in his actions. He shows this side of his nature very soon after he realizes the extent of the catastrophe that has struck the world, and it is particularly evident in the preparations Josella and he make at the apartment. Thus, he judges the importance of their obtaining an apartment for the night as a safe, comfortable place. He also realizes their need for a truck to transport supplies. Further, when Josella draws his attention to the signal beam from the university, he wisely postpones their attempt to reach the source of the signal until morning, having anticipated the danger and confusion of night travel. However, he does not forget to scratch a mark on the window sill to fix the direction from which the beam has come. Later, when Bill and Josella join Beadley's group, Bill's anti-triffid gear is regarded with some scorn. Indeed, when Beadley's party leaves London, they are apparently so scornful of Bill's equipment that they leave it behind. The increasing number of conflicts with triffids points out the wisdom of Bill's precautions, and Beadley later acknowledges the practical rightness of Bill's action. No more vivid example of Bill's practical sense can be found than in his efficient and successful provision for the safety and health of the group at Shirning Farm. There, he is able to clear a large area of triffids by means of a system of defensive fences. When the triffids pierce the defences, Bill electrifies the barriers, using, for power, the generator he starts working after he arrives at the farm. Finally, in the thrilling events at the end of the novel, it is Bill's ingenuity which enables the Shirning party to escape from Torrence and his men, making possible the flight to the Isle of Wight. Obviously, the novel depends heavily upon the sensible leadership which Bill frequently exercises.

A leader must, of course, be courageous, and Bill Masen possesses courage. He does not hesitate to fight on behalf of the girl being abused by the men in Piccadilly Circus, and acts bravely in his rescue of Josella. Further, his many battles with triffids display the same physical courage. However, his courage is not only physical; it has a firm moral aspect to it. This can be seen in his reaction to the horrifying tragedy of May 8. Lesser men, like the landlord of the Alamein Arms, are broken by the catastrophe; some like Miss Durrant, retreat to the comfort of old hopes; others, like Torrence, impose their own violent solution upon the situation. But Bill responds differently. He laments what is lost, and he feels deeply the suffering that the blinded have to endure. Yet he has the moral courage to find in the tragedy a challenge:

> . . . All the old problems, the stale ones, both personal and general, had been solved by one mighty slash. Heaven alone knew as yet what others might arise— and it looked as though there would be plenty of them—but they would be *new*. I was emerging as my own master, and no longer a cog. It might well be a world full of horrors and dangers that I should have to face, but I could take my own steps to deal with it—I would no longer be shoved hither and thither by forces and interests that I neither understood nor cared about.

This note of welcome to a future holding the possibility of unknown threats is a heroic gesture, revealing a man confident of his ability to triumph over disaster.

Finally, Bill Masen is an appropriate hero for the novel because in many ways he is a conventional young man who has an instinctive respect for traditional values. Thus, it is with a genuine feeling of shock that he observes how quickly tragedy and subsequent chaos lead to the abandonment of civilized behavior. In Soho, he observes people competing with one another for food, and describes it as "a grim business without chivalry." The manner in which the citizens of London are "fast losing ordinary restraints" disturbs him greatly. His own behavior reflects a different attitude. For example, his own description of his past life is that it had been "right-respecting" and "law-abiding." In keeping with that way of living, he finds it difficult to adjust to a new world in which old conventions have been swept away:

> . . . Absurd it undoubtedly was, but I had a very strong sense that the moment I should stove in one of those sheets of plate glass I would leave the old order behind me forever: I should become a looter, a sacker, a low scavenger upon the dead body of the system that had nourished me. Such a foolish niceness of sensibility in a stricken world! And yet it still pleases me to remember that civilized usage did not slide off me at once, and that for a time, at least, I wandered along past displays which made my mouth water while my already obsolete conventions kept me hungry.
>
> The problem resolved itself in a sophistical way after perhaps half a mile. A taxi, after mounting the sidewalk, had finished up with its radiator buried in a pile of delicatessen. That made it seem different from doing my own breaking in. I climbed past the taxi and collected the makings of a good meal. But even then some of the old standards still clung: I conscientiously left a fair price for what I had taken lying on the counter.

Bill's romantic relationship with Josella similarly illustrates the value he places upon old conventions. When they spend their first night together at the apartment, Bill is still mindful of the proprieties of the situation, and even offers to find a second apartment for Josella. Later, after Dr. Vorless, the sociologist in Beadley's party, outlines the new social organization which would be initiated, Bill is obviously somewhat startled at the suggestion that he would have living with him, in addition to

Josella, two blind women, with whom he would father children. Josella is able to accept the proposal calmly. In contrast, Bill at first dismisses it as "crazy" and "unnatural." The reaction is neither more nor less than that which might be expected from Bill. He is not by nature a revolutionary or a radical. He is rather, a sensible, conventional, law-abiding citizen, whose life has been disrupted dramatically by a catastrophe of global proportions.

In summary, it is a fitting conclusion that Bill Masen is, in most respects, a typical hero. His courage, his resourcefulness and his innate goodness are conventional qualities that one might expect in a hero. In a sense, what makes him different is his ordinariness. He is a typical man, and not an exceptional superman.

The Landlord of the Alamein Arms

The landlord is a very minor character in the novel. A "large-bellied, red-faced man with a graying walrus mustache," he is discovered, drunken and alone, by Bill, in the pub which stood almost opposite the gates of the hospital. The man is deliberately drinking in order to achieve the courage to commit suicide. As he explains to Bill, his wife has already gassed herself and their children, following their blindness. He has not had the courage to join her. Now, he is systematically seeking that courage from the bottles in the bar. As Bill leaves the pub, the landlord begins to climb upstairs to join his wife and children in the relief of death.

The incident involving the landlord is very brief, but it does serve a number of purposes in the story:

1. It acquaints the reader with some of the implications of what is happening. The extent—or even the nature—of the tragedy is not yet fully revealed. Thus, the horror of what happens to the man is a grim foreshadowing of the horrors to come.

2. Bill's encounter with the landlord supplies the hero with the first firm clue of the extent of the catastrophe. From the landlord, Bill receives his first intimation that everyone is blind.

3. The disturbing encounter with this man provides some of the motivation for Bill's decision to direct his steps toward the center of London and, so, is the first stage of a grim voyage of discovery.

Bill's Father

This is another very minor character. Mr. Masen seems to be remarkable chiefly for the contrast he offers to his son. Bill's father, unlike Bill, has an aptitude for figures, and is an accountant in the internal revenue department. Obviously a typical civil servant, he wants his son to pursue a conventional, secure career, and is disappointed when Bill does no better than to find employment with the Arctic & European Oil Company.

Mr. and Mrs. Masen are killed in the crash of a holiday airbus, before the events which provide the action for *The Day of the Triffids*.

Umberto Christoforo Palanguez

Umberto is a pilot of Latin descent who revolutionizes the edible oil industry when he approaches the Arctic & European Fish Oil Company with a sample of triffid oil. The company pays him an enormous sum of money to obtain a supply of the seeds of the unidentified vegetable, which he says is to be found in Russia. What happens to Umberto after that is only speculation. It seems that he flew to Russia to acquire the seeds, but he never does return. Possibly, his aircraft is shot down by the Russians, spilling his load of seeds over the earth. Thus, according to Bill's guess, Umberto might have been the one man responsible for the spreading of the triffid plants into Europe and the rest of the world.

Walter Lucknor

Walter, one of Bill's colleagues at the Arctic & European Oil Company, is one of the more interesting minor characters. He is an unusual man, for he has few formal qualifications for his job. As Bill expresses it, he "knew little of agriculture, less of business, and lacked the qualifications for lab work." However, his one outstanding quality is his natural understanding of triffids; as Bill observes, "he had a kind of inspired knack with them."

Walter formulates a number of theories and makes a number of discoveries about the triffids:

1. He is the first to suggest to Bill that the rattling of the triffids' sticks is a form of communication.

2. He interprets this communication as evidence of some form of triffid intelligence.

111

3. Signs of triffid intelligence leads him to talk of the plants in terms of their being competitors to man. Having observed that the triffids usually aim for the head in directing their stings, he concludes that they realize that vision is the source of man's supremacy over them.

4. He establishes the fact that, deprived of its "sticks," a triffid gradually deteriorates.

5. He also establishes that the infertility rate of triffid seeds is in the region of 95 per cent.

Walter Lucknor appears only briefly in the pages of the novel, yet his contribution to triffid mythology and fact is important. In addition, his healthy respect for the triffids is the source of much of Bill's later care and caution in facing the new, blind world after May 8.

Josella Playton

Bill first encounters Josella when he rescues her from the blind man who holds her captive. She is captured by the man while she is seeking a doctor to assist her father who, like many others, awakened to blindness on May 8.

At that time, she is about twenty-four years of age. Her clothes, Bill notices, are good, and her appearance seems to indicate that she lives prosperously.

At the age of nineteen, Josella almost marries. Her choice of a husband—a "sort of cross between a spiv and a lizard"— enrages her family. Thus, she leaves her family to live with a girlfriend, and her family, in retaliation, cuts off her allowance. Shortage of money makes her decide to write a book, *Sex Is My Adventure*. It is, really, according to Josella, a "harmless little book," a mixture of "green-sophisticated and pink-romantic, with patches of schoolgirly purple." But it is the title which sells the book. Two large libraries ban it, with the result that sales boom. Josella becomes a kind of notorious celebrity and, to protect her privacy, she is obliged to move back to her home. She learns to regret having written the book, for it gives her an unwelcome and unjustified reputation. When tragedy strikes the world, she is busy writing another book, *Here the Forsaken*, in an attempt to "balance things up again."

Josella accompanies Bill after her rescue, and they both join Beadley's party. Like Bill, Josella is kidnapped by Coker's men, and only escapes when the plague afflicts the blind people.

She intends to return to the university to look for Bill, but is frightened off by the sound of a shot. Ironically, the shot is fired by Bill, though she is unaware of his presence at the time. Leaving London, she goes to Shirning Farm, in the Sussex Downs, which is owned by the Brents, who are friends of hers. During her years there with Bill, she gives birth to two children. She later escapes, with all the people at Shirning, to the Isle of Wight.

Josella, of course, provides the romantic interest in the novel. Her love affair with, and eventual marriage to, Bill is an important sub-plot. However, Josella is an interesting character in her own right.

On most occasions, she appears to be a conventional, female figure. Her appearance, especially her fingernails which "showed a length more decorative than practical," is decidedly feminine. So are her emotional responses, particularly in the early stages of the novel. When Bill rescues her from her blind captor, she bursts into tears of relief and, after she does some repair work on her appearance, she, in Bill's words, "approximated . . . the film director's idea of the heroine after a roughhouse." By her own confession, her behavior during the incident is less than rational; she is rather like "a girl in a Victorian melodrama." In the conflict with the triffids at her home, Josella behaves no differently: she cries out hysterically for Bill to drive away from the house. At the apartment, Josella's conventional femininity is expressed even more emphatically. She loves the luxury of the apartment, choosing for herself a room "rampant with all the most aggressive manifestations of femininity."

Yet, there is another aspect of Josella that deserves consideration. It appears gradually in the novel, beginning with their stay at the apartment. While Bill prepares their dinner on the first evening, Josella enters the room and her appearance startles and surprises Bill, as well it might:

> . . . She was wearing a long, pretty frock of palest blue georgette with a little jacket of white fur. In a pendant on a simple chain a few blue-white diamonds flashed; the stones that gleamed in her ear-clips were smaller but as fine in color. Her hair and her face might have been fresh from a beauty parlor. She

crossed the room with a flicker of silver slippers and a glimpse of gossamer stockings.

The dress might be regarded as typical of the "old" Josella, the girl who displayed frivolous femininity, but on this occasion it is symbolic as a farewell gesture to the old way of life. It can also be interpreted as a farewell gesture to conventional femininity. After that moment, Josella seems to become more decisive, shrewd and practical. When Bill first met her, he had observed that she looked "as if she had strength if it were necessary." After that evening in the apartment, Josella reveals more and more of her strength. Thus, at the meeting held by Beadley's group, it is she—and not Bill—who realizes the full implications of Dr. Vorless's plans for the party's social organization. She is rational enough to accept those plans, appreciating their logic, and persuades Bill of their rightness. Later, when captured by Coker's people, she forcefully persuades her captors to take off her bonds. On arriving at Shirning Farm, the place of refuge she had suggested to Bill, she takes charge of the household, spending her days working, learning and improvising. All of this suggests a character far different from that of the woman Bill rescued. It is clear that there are resources within Josella sufficient to meet the demands which the emergency presents.

Of course, it must be admitted that there is little depth to the character of Josella. By and large, it is a conventional picture that Wyndham presents. However, the occasional flashes of humor she displays and the suggestions of strength we are given do make her an interesting character in the novel.

Wilfred Coker

Coker first appears in the novel in front of the gates of the university. About thirty years of age, "with a straight, narrow nose and rather bony features," he possesses an intensity of manner that is more remarkable than his physical appearance.

Coker reacts to the catastrophe in a way that contrasts sharply with the reaction of Beadley's group. Stressing the need for survival, the latter does not want to be burdened with blind people. Coker, on the other hand, acts with compassion. He seeks to give leadership to the blind. For this reason, he leads them to the university gates and, in seeking help, declares his views strongly and bluntly:

> "Now listen to me," he said angrily. "These people here have got just as much bloody right to live as you have, haven't they? It's not their fault they're blind, is it? It's nobody's fault—but it's going to be your fault if they starve, and you know it."

When his pleading fails, he devises and carries out successfully the plan for kidnapping sighted people from the university to lead groups of the blind. By means of his scheme, Josella and Bill become captives. Coker divides his people into groups, each one led by a sighted person. Each group is assigned an area in which they are to find the means of survival. In theory, the plan is excellent, however, from a long-term point of view, the scheme is a mistake. Helping the blind is, at best, only a temporary measure that does not recognize sufficiently the demands of the different world of the future. The unusual sickness ends Coker's scheme abruptly.

After many of his people die from the mysterious sickness, Coker returns to the university, where he meets Bill once more. Together, they leave London to search for Beadley. When they arrive at Tynsham to discover only Miss Durrant and her party, Coker is dismayed by their inattention to practical matters. His blunt observations earn him the anger of Miss Durrant. Therefore, when Bill leaves Tynsham, still seeking Beadley, Coker leaves, also. Coker later returns to Tynsham with Stephen Brennell and his companions, for he believes that, with practical help, Miss Durrant's party might offer good chances of survival. However, a few days after his return, the sickness strikes the community. Coker tries to organize the people to battle it, but the task is hopeless. In Devonshire, Coker tries to survive in much the same way as Bill and his friends do. Finally, when Beadley's group discovers him, Coker takes his people to the Isle of Wight.

Coker is one of the most interesting minor characters in *The Day of the Triffids*. Describing himself with amusing scorn as a "hybrid," he at first encounters some difficulty in finding his place in society. He, therefore, gravitates toward attending protest meetings of various kinds, which brings him to the attention of people better educated than himself. This stimulates an interest in more education, and he attends evening classes. In this process, he discovers and refines his ability to address audiences in a way that they understand and appreciate. Thus, he makes himself, by his own description, bilingual; he is able to assume a common language when it is needed. This was his way of beating the English class system, and it works, for he "made out quite nicely in the orating business." In fact, public speaking saves Coker's sight and, perhaps, his life, because, following a meeting on May 7, he hides from the police in a cellar and so escapes the blindness that most others suffer.

In his concern for the blind people, Coker shows himself to be a man of compassion, in spite of the cynicism apparent in his own account of his life before the catastrophe. His compassion proves to be directed toward a mistaken solution; nonetheless, it is an attractive quality in the man. The same compassion is evident in his reaction to Miss Durrant and her group. His criticisms of their organization are delivered bluntly, but his attitude is only a sign of his concern. Later, when telling Stephen Brennell about the Tynsham community, his concern is evident:

> I've been thinking of that place Bill and I saw at Tynsham. We've told you about it. The woman who is trying to run it wanted help, and she wanted it badly. She has about fifty or sixty people on her hands, and a dozen or so of them able to see. That way she can't do it. She knows she can't—but she wasn't going to admit it to us. She wasn't going to put herself in our debt by asking us to stay. But she'd be very glad if we were to go back there after all and ask to be admitted.

On returning to Tynsham, he makes valiant efforts to save the community by organizing the quarantining of the sick when the sickness comes. In the years that follow, he obviously fights bravely to protect the group that he leads. Thus, Coker is clearly a gallant man, moved by a genuine concern for others, in spite of his own cynical talk about himself.

Above all, Coker is a likeable man. Shrewd and intelligent, he carefully safeguards his health in face of the disease that afflicts those around him. Also, with complete sincerity, he is able to admit his fault when he is wrong, as he does to Bill when talking of the failure of the scheme to enable the blind to survive:

> "I'd got it wrong," he repeated. "I thought I was the one who was taking it seriously—but I wasn't taking it seriously enough. I couldn't believe that it would last, or that some kind of help wouldn't show up. Europe, Asia, America—think of America smitten like this! But they must be. If they weren't, they'd have been over here, helping out and getting the place straight— that's the way it'd take them. No, I reckon your lot understood it better from the start."

In terms of the plot, Coker's contribution is twofold:

1. He is the cause of the adventures of Bill that lead to his separation from Josella's and Beadley's party. Thus, Coker's actions are the reason for the central section of the narrative, in which Bill undertakes his search for Josella.

2. Coker represents the working out of one possible response to the tragedy. It is an attractive response, since it involves caring for those who obviously need care. In this respect, it contrasts with the solution proposed by Beadley and his group. However, in part, the novel stresses the need for new ways to meet new demands. Old customs and old precepts and old laws are, it suggests, inadequate to meet the bewildering challenges to be faced. Clearly, in Coker we see that compassion is, by itself, inadequate. A new approach is needed, and Beadley is to provide it.

The Colonel

The colonel—his name is only mentioned once as being Jaques—is in charge of the practical details involved in the organization of Beadley's party.

He is "a chubby man just turned fifty or thereabout." A brisk, healthy looking, efficient man, his appearance reveals his character:

> ... His hair was plentiful but well-trimmed, and gray. His mustache matched it and looked as if no single hair would dare to break the ranks. His com-

plexion was so pink, healthy, and fresh that it might have belonged to a much younger man; his mind, I discovered later, had never ceased to do so. He was sitting behind a table with quantities of paper arranged on it in mathematically exact blocks and an unsoiled sheet of pink blotting paper placed squarely before him.

Typically, when Bill and Josella are first brought to him, he speaks of the need for system and organization, and carefully makes a note of their names and addresses. His attitude prompts Josella to remark jokingly that he forgot to ask for their references!

As expected, when the colonel addresses the meeting of Beadley's group, he is practical and factual. He stresses the need to leave the city and to gather supplies sufficient for independent existence for one year. Though his practical manner has a reassuring effect, Bill thinks at the time that the colonel is making a mistake in not informing the gathering of the location of the place of retreat.

Beadley's party establishes themselves in Oxfordshire. After a year, however, both Beadley and the colonel realize the hopelessness of fences as a protection against the triffids. The decision to move to the Isle of Wight follows and, presumably, the colonel is still one of the community at the end of the novel.

Michael Beadley

Beadley's appearance offers a sharp contrast to that of the colonel:

. . . He was lean, tall, broad-shouldered, and slightly stooping, with some of the air of an athlete run to books. In repose his face took on an expression of mild gloom from the darkness of his large eyes, but it was seldom that one had a glimpse of it in repose. The occasional streaks of gray in his hair helped very little in judging his age. He might have been anywhere between thirty-five and fifty. His obvious weariness just then made an estimate still more difficult. By his looks, he must have been up all night; nevertheless, he greeted us cheerfully. . . .

In his own way, Beadley is obviously just as efficient as the colonel, though his words and actions are not so abrupt. His major contribuion to the community he leads is in the philosophical basis for the group. He explains with great clarity the dimensions of the tragedy which confronts them, likening it to the Great Flood of man's mythological past. However, he insists, what had happened is not the end of everything. People, he says, must patiently begin again, and begin with hope, for their assets are considerable:

> . . . The Earth is intact, unscarred, still fruitful. It can provide us with food and raw materials. We have repositories of knowledge that can teach us to do anything that has been done before—though there are some things that may be better unremembered. And we have the means, the health, and the strength to begin to build again.

The effectiveness of Beadley's leadership can be judged from the success of the community he establishes on the Isle of Wight, according to the account of it given by Ivan Simpson. The triffids are eliminated on the Isle of Wight, and another community starts cleaning up the Channel Isles. With the lessening of danger, time is found to undertake research aimed at finding a scientific method of destroying the triffids. This success enables Bill to write hopefully, at the end of the novel, of the future day that would see men returning to Britain to drive the triffids back.

Sandra Telmont
Sandra Telmont is the "professional remembrancer" of Beadley's group. In this capacity, her functions seem to be those of an executive secretary. For example, she organizes the members of the group at the beginning of their conference.

Elspeth Cary
Elspeth, "a young woman in a brick-red lumber jacket and an elegant pair of green trousers," is the "official record" of Beadley's community. She eventually writes what Bill describes as an excellent history of the colony on the Isle of Wight.

119

Ivan Simpson

Ivan is the pilot in Beadley's community. His arrival in a helicopter interrupts a conversation between Bill and Josella, and Miss Cary. He is not mentioned in any detail in the novel until he arrives at Shirning Farm to offer to take Bill and his friends to the Isle of Wight. He is the means chosen by Wyndham to inform Bill of the adventures of the Beadley group after their departure from London. He also tells of the experiences of Coker following his stay with the Tynsham community.

Miss Berr

Miss Berr is a highly qualified nurse, who supplies the need of Beadley's party for someone with medical knowledge. She inoculates the members of the group against a variety of diseases. To judge from her blushing participation in the conference at the university, she would seem to be a rather shy girl.

Dr. E.Y. Vorless, D.Sc.

Dr. Vorless, a professor of sociology at the University of Kingston, is "an elderly man of ugly but benign aspect who wore gold-rimmed spectacles and had fine white hair trimmed to a rather political length." He explains to the conference the social principles on which Beadley's community will be founded.

Almost seventy years of age, he emphasizes the need for new customs to meet new conditions. The old way of life is gone, he says. As a result, the task facing them is basic: "we have now to find out what mode of life is best suited to the new." That mode of life, he continues, will elevate the importance of one principle—that the race is worth preserving. In speaking of their roles in the future, he declares that the men must work and the women must have babies. Because of this, the community will be able to support a limited number of women who cannot see, but they will not be able to afford men who cannot see.

Dr. Vorless's final words to the meeting provide a neat summary of his sociological message:

Not one of us is going to recapture the conditions we have lost. What we offer is a busy life in the best conditions we can contrive, and the happiness which will come of achievement against odds. In return we ask willingness and fruitfulness. There is no compulsion. The choice is yours. Those to whom our offer does not appeal are at perfect liberty to go elsewhere and start a separate community on such lines as they prefer.

Miss Durrant

Miss Durrant is the "tall, dark, purposeful-looking, youngish woman" who opposes the views of Dr. Vorless at the conference of Beadley's group. She equates his views with advocating free love, and upholds the marriage law as "still God's law, and the law of decency."

Bill does not see Miss Durrant again until he reaches Tynsham in his search for Beadley. She has established a community of her own there, organized, she explains, according to Christian principles:

> . . . This is a clean, decent community with standards—Christian standards—and we intend to uphold them. We have no place here for people of loose views. Decadence, immorality, and lack of faith were responsible for most of the world's ills. It is the duty of those of us who have been spared to see that we build a society where that does not happen again. The cynical and the clever-clever will find they are not wanted here, no matter what brilliant theories they may put forward to disguise their licentiousness and their materialism. We are a Christian community, and we intend to remain so.

Miss Durrant's point of view is proven to be a mistake in the novel. Like Coker, she learns that compassion is not enough to meet and conquer the challenges of a world that has changed drastically. Thus, her action in welcoming blind people into her community is admirable and generous. Nevertheless, from a practical point of view it is also unrealistic and impractical. New ways of living demand a vital contribution from everyone, so that the many blind people in her group are undoubtedly a liability rather than an asset.

121

To give Miss Durrant credit, she is aware of the difficulties her position causes. Thus, in spite of early antagonism, she recognizes the worth of Coker. She is unable to express her appreciation for the practical help that Bill and Coker represent, but she is very much aware that she needs them. Her dedication to her principles is evident in her final action: she decides to remain to help the unfortunate. Her dedication to her Christian beliefs thus seems to have found its ultimate expression in self-sacrifice.

Miss Durrant's one puzzling action is that of misleading Bill and Coker about the direction Beadley's group had taken. She thinks they have gone to Beaminster, whereas she knows, in fact, that they have travelled into Oxfordshire. This deliberate lie is hardly in accord with her Christian principles, and may be explained by the desperate situation in which she finds herself. She needs the help Bill and Coker could give, but she is too proud to ask them to remain. Her lie, then, may be an attempt to ensure their return to Tynsham after a fruitless search for Beadley.

The Young Man with the Pistol

The name of this redheaded young man is never revealed, and he appears very briefly in the story. Bill meets him while leading a party of blind men in search of food. The young man seems to be giving the same kind of leadership as Bill.

However, the young man's reaction is different. On seeing Bill's party, he draws a pistol from his pocket and begins shooting, killing one of Bill's captors. He follows Bill's men until one of them drops to the ground, apparently overcome by the disease. The young man acts with deliberation when he shoots the fallen man.

The young man's presence in the novel helps to underline the growing violence witnessed in the disrupted city.

The Young Girl who Committed Suicide

This girl is one of the group of blind people for whom Bill is made responsible by Coker. She is young—under twenty, in Bill's estimation—and pretty.

Her role in the novel adds a dimension of tragic pathos. She comes to Bill's room after the plague has afflicted her companions, and offers herself to him in return for his staying with them. Her appearance reminds Bill of the sweetness of the life that has now vanished, and of the harsh demands that lie ahead. He, of course, rejects her offer, the sadness of the moment bringing tears to his eyes, and assures her that he will remain. Unfortunately, Bill discovers the next morning that the girl has also been stricken by the plague. He complies sorrowfully with her request for a drug to end the misery of her life. However, the memory of her selflessness remains with him:

> I looked down at her as she lay. I felt very angry with the stupidity of death. A thousand would have said: "Take me with you"; but she had said: "Stay with us."
>
> And I never even knew her name.

Stephen Brennell

Brennell is a fair-haired young man who is a member of the stock exchange. With a voluptuous but rather vapid girlfriend, and being a man with a passionate desire to own a radio store of his own, he begins to fortify Charcott Old House against the triffids and against human intruders.

Brennell, armed with a rifle, stops Bill and Coker in the village of Beaminster. He becomes friendly when he learns that the newcomers do not have violent intentions. During the next few days, Brennell and his friends assist in the search for Beadley, even obtaining a helicopter for greater efficiency.

When the search for Beadley proves unsuccessful, Brennell's intention is to remain at Charcott Old House. However, Coker impresses upon him the need for belonging to a larger community which could, at the very least, support "the leader, the teacher, and the doctor." Consequently, Brennell and his friends return to Tynsham with Coker, while Bill continues his travels to find Josella. Neither Brennell nor his friends are mentioned subsequently in the novel.

Susan

Bill meets Susan during his journey to the Sussex Downs. Only nine or ten years of age, she is the only survivor in her village. Tearfully, she seeks Bill's aid for her brother, Tommy, who is about four years of age. The little boy, Bill sees, is beyond help; he has been killed by a triffid.

Susan, in spite of her age, displays remarkable courage. Both of her parents have disappeared, presumably killed by triffids, and she has been left in sole charge of her brother. She has even gone to the village store for food, and has also sought to make Tommy wary of the triffids.

She proves to be a valuable companion for Bill. She is the first to notice the light from Shirning Farm. In later years, she helps to look after Josella's children. She also notices a significant fact which Bill has overlooked: that the triffids are attracted by the noise from Bill's farm machinery.

Dennis Brent

Dennis Brent owns Shirning Farm. When the catastrophe strikes, he is at the farm with his wife, Mary, and three friends, Joan and Ted Danton, and Joyce Taylor. All five are blinded. The Dentons subsequently leave the farmhouse and never return, presumably they have been killed by the triffids. Only the Brents and Joyce remain when Josella arrives at the farm.

Dennis is obviously a man of courage. He gropes his way to the village, using uncoiled rope to guide him, and he seeks to be helpful to Bill, in spite of the handicap of blindness.

Mary Brent bears a child during the early days at Shirning Farm.

Mr. Torrence

Mr. Torrence describes himself as the commander of the emergency council for the southeastern region of Britain. As such, he is the representative of a group that seeks to impose a military solution upon the chaos that followed May 8. Their headquarters is at Brighton, but the plague forces them to disperse into smaller units. Thus, they intend to take over Shirning Farm, and send in seventeen more blind people, who will be looked after by Bill and Josella. Susan will be taken away until she becomes old enough to look after her own group of ten blind people.

Torrence's plans horrify the Shirning Farm group. Most of all, they are horrified at the tyrannical, military aspects of Torrence's scheme. An armed, mobile squad of police would impose law and order, to the end that one day Britain might become the dominant power in Europe. The threat posed by Torrence precipitates the flight of the Shirning party to the Isle of Wight.

Setting

The events of *The Day of the Triffids* take place in southern England, but it is the setting in time that is more important. However, much of the effectiveness of the story springs from the fact that that world of the future is not so very different from the world we live in today.

To begin with, the world of Bill's story does not present us with any startling or unusual advantages in technology. True, travel is apparently swift and easy, but the means of travel are the same as those we know—roads, automobiles, trains, ships and airplanes. Moreover, even the anti-triffid weapons which are devised are simple variations of a bow and arrow. Certainly, daily life is untouched by advances in technology. For example, when Bill runs Shirning Farm, he still employs conventional tractors and powers the farm with an electrical generator.

Similarly, the world of the novel is little different from ours in a political sense. The same nations seem to be striving and competing in the same way as they do in our time. Peace does reign, but it is of the uneasy kind that we know now. Humans have satellites circling the globe, as we have presently.

The major difference between that world and our own seems to be the deadly load carried by the satellites. Apparently, from what Bill says, at least one of them contains some material having sufficient radiation to cause blindness. By accident or design, it had unleashed its horror suddenly upon the world between May 7 and May 8. The catastrophe escalates to horrifying proportions through the presence of the triffids which, possibly through some strange mutations, had developed characteristics which enable them to threaten the very existence of the human race.

It is significant that, in painting a picture of the future, Wyndham chooses a world so familiar to us. In the first place, it undoubtedly helps the reader to accept more easily the relevance of the story to his own world. Undistracted by technological novelties and undisturbed by strange concepts, the reader can thus focus his attention upon the ideas being presented, rather than upon alluring attractions that are just entertaining. This observation about the setting leads, in the second place, to a conclusion about the novel which is hardly surprising: that Wyndham is actually writing about our world, and not really about a strange world of the future at all. The technique is not new. George Orwell, in *1984*, did the same thing; he was not writing about the future but, rather, about his own anxious world of the forties, with its dangerous implications for the future. In exactly the same way, Wyndham is providing a warning. He examines human nature and human life as we know them today, in order to explore the implications of man's behavior for the future.

Structure

The structure of a novel is, basically, the term used to describe the writer's ordering of the events in his story. That concept is important, for it emphasizes the fact that no novel is simply a slice of life recorded by a novelist. Life in a novel is not real life, for the writer engages in a complex process of selection, editing and ordering in order to emphasize the characters, events and themes that he wishes to assume importance for the reader. This process is, of course, quite different from the common process of living in everyday experience. In daily life, many of our thoughts, words and experiences are trivial and insignificant. In fact, if those aspects of our normal daily life were recorded on paper, they would seem bewildering and incoherent to a reader. Thus, formulating a story and inventing characters, the novelist draws upon his experience of human living, but he fashions his creation according to a preconceived plan. That plan provides the structure of the novel. Obviously, understanding that plan can give the reader important clues about the novelist's purpose in writing his book.

In order to understand the structure of *The Day of the Triffids*, it is necessary to have a clear view of the novel as a whole. To this end, the contents of the chapters may be briefly summarized, as follows:

> "The End Begins": The central character, William Masen, awakens to a world suddenly and mysteriously afflicted by blindness.
>
> "The Coming of the Triffids": The origin, history and nature of the triffids is explained.
>
> "The Groping City": The narrator, wandering in London, begins to realize the extent of his plight.
>
> "Shadows Before": The effect of the catastrophe upon the people of London is described, and Masen first meets Josella Playton.
>
> "A Light in the Night": Bill and Josella, preparing to flee from London, see a signal light at the university tower.
>
> "Rendezvous": Bill and Josella are united with Beadley's group. Coker appears in the novel for the first time.

"Conference": Beadley's group holds a meeting in which their plans for the future are revealed.

"Frustration": By means of a trick engineered by Coker, Bill and Josella are forced to lead groups of blind people and are, thus, separated from Beadley's group and from one another. A mysterious plague enables Bill to escape.

"Evacuation": Bill returns to the university, but finds that Beadley's party has left, apparently for Tynsham. Coker joins him and the two leave London to go to Tynsham.

"Tynsham": Miss Durrant's group is in residence at Tynsham. There is no news of Josella or of Beadley.

"And Farther On": Bill, still thinking of Josella, and Coker, despairing of the future of the disorganized Tynsham community, leave to search for Beadley.

"Dead End": Bill and Coker encounter and join a small group made up of Stephen Brennell, a girl and the radio enthusiast. After fruitless searches for Beadley, the rest of the party decide to go to Tynsham, while Bill proceeds to the Sussex Downs in search of Josella.

"Journey in Hope": On his journey, Bill meets the child, Susan, whom he takes with him. He is reunited with Josella at Shirning Farm.

"Shirning": the previous experiences of Josella and the others at Shirning are explained. On a visit to Tynsham, Bill discovers that the community has disappeared.

"World Narrowing": the difficulties of life at Shirning are described. The decay of London is revealed. Josella's first baby is born. The difficulties with the triffids become acute. Bill and Josella see Ivan Simpson's helicopter fly overhead.

"Contact": Simpson gives an account of Beadley's community on the Isle of Wight, where Coker is also to be found. The Shirning group decides to join Beadley at the end of the summer.

"Strategic Withdrawal": Shirning Farm is commandeered by the emergency council. The Shirning group escape to join Beadley. In an epilogue, Bill explains what the future holds.

Such a bird's-eye view of the novel brings out clearly, in the first place, the basically chronological nature of Wyndham's narrative. As the second chapter ("The Coming of the Triffids") and the last chapter ("Strategic Withdrawal") make clear, the story is, as it unfolds for the reader, being told by Bill Masen. He, living with the community on the Isle of Wight, is recollecting and recording the events of the past, beginning with that fateful Wednesday, May 8. The tale unfolds in a logical time sequence, following Bill's adventures in London, his experiences with Coker, his reunion with Josella, his life at Shirning Farm and his eventual escape to the Isle of Wight. In all of these twists and turns of the plot, the element of time is not neglected. The passing of time is clearly indicated throughout. The chapter entitled "World Narrowing" is a good example of this firm chronology. There, we are informed explicitly of the time sequence of a variety of events:

1. Bill began to build a protective fence against the triffids *within a week* of his visit to the plague-ridden Tynsham community.

2. Bill let a *whole year* pass before he visited London again.

3. His second visit to London took place *a year later*.

4. *Later on* he visited London for a third time.

5. A *week later*, Josella re-visited London for the first—and last—time.

6. At *the end of his fourth year* at Shirning, Bill visited London for the last time.

7. David was born *in November of the second year* at Shirning.

8. *Not long after that*, Josella drew Bill's attention to the intensified activity of the triffids.

9. Bill's devices to trap and destroy the triffids were tried *for a year or more* before the triffids first broke into the compound.

10. The second break-in occurred *four months* after the first.

11. They saw Simpson's helicopter "*in the summer which began our sixth year.*"

This chapter is only one example which illustrates vividly the chronological technique of the narrative. There are innumerable other parts of the novel that betray the same careful attention to time, and attention which focusses not only on the passing of years, but on the passing of days and even of hours. This systematic chronology, of course, enables Wyndham to achieve a number of objectives. In the first place, it gives the narrative the credibility of a journal. It is Bill's record of his experiences and, thus, it is in keeping with the nature of the narrative to have the sequence of events delineated clearly. In the second place, the firm chronology helps to achieve credibility to the science fiction aspect of the novel. That credibility is not easy to achieve for the writer of science fiction. He is drawing a portrait of a future world, but that future world must be sufficiently credible to attract the interest and gain the understanding of the reader. Wyndham's scrupulous attention to the chronology helps to capture the interest and understanding of the reader, leading him to believe, for a while at least, that the events of the book just might be possible.

However, the major importance of the chronology of the narrative lies elsewhere. It gives an important clue to the nature of the novel as a whole. It is clearly an adventure story, with the major emphasis on the plot. Other aspects of the work—for example, characterization and setting—are secondary to the account of the adventures of Bill Masen. True, it is an unusual adventure story. It is set in the world of the future, a world beset by strange adversity which the hero must struggle with and conquer. Yet the adventure story is never lost from sight. The strange coincidences in the novel, the sudden encounters with new people, the frequent confrontations with danger, the thrilling escapes which often take place—all of these elements are a fundamental part of the narrative and emphasize the prime importance of the plot. *The Day of the Triffids*, as we see from its chronological structure is, at heart, a thrilling adventure story.

Nevertheless, there are two other important aspects of the novel which help to create its structure. The first of these is the sub-plot involving Josella. This sub-plot, first of all, provides the motivation for the middle portion of the narrative, when Bill is looking for Josella. The separation of Bill and Josella, and Bill's subsequent search for her, occupies six chapters— "Frustration," "Evacuation," "Tynsham," "—And Farther On," "Dead End" and "Journey in Hope." In actual fact, the entire relationship in the novel is structured precisely to form a three-act drama, which might be described according to the following scheme:

1. *The Relationship Begins*, as revealed in "Shadows Before," "A Light in the Night," "Rendezvous" and "Conference." Significantly, this part of the story ends with the feelings of love between Bill and Josella explicitly expressed:

> "Josella," I said.
> "M'm?" she replied, scarcely emerging from her thought.
> "Josella," I said again. "Er—those babies. I'd be—er—I'd be sort of terribly proud and happy if they could be mine as well as yours."
> She sat quite still for a moment, saying nothing. Then she turned her head. The moon-light was glinting on her fair hair, but her face and eyes were in shadow. I waited, with a hammered and slightly sick feeling inside me. She said, with surprising calm:
> "Thank you, Bill dear. I think I would too."
> I sighed. The hammering did not ease up much, and I saw that my hand was trembling as it reached for hers.

In this way, the romantic conclusion of the first section of the story provides a fitting prologue for the section in which the love of Bill and Josella encounters disappointments and frustrations.

2. *The Search*, narrated in "Frustration," "Evacuation," "Tynsham," "—And Farther On," "Dead End," and "Journey in Hope."

3. *Reunion and Renewal*, contained in "Shirning," "World Narrowing," "Contact" and "Strategic Withdrawal." These final four chapters of the novel show the lovers together once more, establish their marriage, portray their life at Shirning and sketch their future together.

The precision of the scheme is obvious, because the prologue of the sub-plot, called here "The Relationship Begins," occupies four chapters, the middle section encompasses six chapters, and the final section, called here "Reunion and Renewal," covers—like the prologue—four chapters. This little "drama," of course, contributes to the human interest of the novel, and provides the motivation for many of Bill's actions.

Another unifying thread in the narrative is supplied by the sub-plot involving Beadley and his group (Miss Durrant's party can be regarded as a minor aspect of Beadley's group). In one way, their story diverts the direction of the main plot of the book because, in the fifth chapter, "A Light in the Night," Josella had already mentioned the farmhouse in the Sussex Downs, yet it is not until the thirteenth chapter, "Journey in Hope," that Bill arrives at Shirning Farm. Between these two chapters, there are two others, "Rendezvous" and "Conference," which are almost entirely devoted to Beadley's group, and a number of others which feature Bill's search for Beadley and Josella. Of course, that does not mean that the Beadley sub-plot is irrevelant to the main plot. On the contrary, it makes four major contributions to the novel:

1. The story of Beadley establishes Bill's connection with other survivors. This is an indispensable contribution, for when the novel begins, Bill is alone. In fact, one of his most vivid and overwhelming feelings is that of loneliness, as he explains when he first walks the streets of London after the tragedy:

> . . . I was feeling somewhat restored, but curiously detached now, and rudderless. I had no glimmering of a plan, and in face of what I had at last begun to perceive as a vast and not merely local catastrophe, I was still too stunned to begin to reason one out. What plan could there be to deal with such a thing? I felt forlorn, cast into desolation, and yet not quite real, not quite myself here and now.

When Bill meets Josella, and they both encounter Beadley, Bill is no longer "detached." The plans of the group mean that he is no longer "rudderless." The forces of his reason begin to work, and his sense of "desolation" wanes.

2. The introduction of Beadley's group enables Wyndham to move the action of the novel out of London swiftly and easily. The cause of the changes of scene which follow is Bill's search for Beadley. This movement of physical location is, naturally, important. By means of the change, the novelist is able to show the extent of the tragedy which visited Britain.

3. The existence of the Beadley party makes more vivid the presentation of the various responses to the central catastrophe in the novel. His is the group that understands the extent of the tragedy most clearly, except for his first inattention to the threat of the triffids. Thus, though at first Coker's work with blind people may seem to be more appealing in humanitarian terms than Beadley's organization, the inadequacy and ultimate folly of Coker's response is demonstrated in the contrast with Beadley's concepts. Similarly, Miss Durrant's basic weakness is highlighted by the contrast with Beadley's party. Like Coker's initial response, Miss Durrant's reaction to the tragedy tends to ignore the full horror and urgency of the situation. Vague humanitarianism and a sentimental clinging to old ways are, the contrast tells us, inadequate and, ultimately, disastrous. On the other hand, Torrence's group, the emergency council, ignores the human element almost entirely, for its ultimate objective is political power rather than human survival.

4. Finally, the story of Beadley's group points the narrative toward the future. It enables the novelist to indicate the solution to the problem posed by the catastrophe that had gripped the world. Of great importance in that solution is the principle of survival. The race, as Dr. Vorless explained, must continue, even, for example, at the expense of the sacrifice of monogamous marriage. Yet, human qualities would not be entirely lost. Men would direct their intelligence and knowledge toward finding a weapon to destroy the triffids, and the blind of the community would not be abandoned. Human reason, applied in practical ways, would ensure the future, as Dr. Vorless emphasized when he declared: "Not one of us is going to recapture the conditions we have lost. What we offer is a busy life in the best conditions we can contrive, and the happiness which will come of achievement against odds."

Finally, two minor narrative devices contribute to the structure of *The Day of the Triffids*. The first of these is Wyndham's frequent use of startling and unexpected events to move the story swiftly. Many examples of the technique can be found:

— the sudden scream which leads to Bill's meeting with Josella ("Shadows Before")
— the sighting of the signal beam from the university tower ("A Light in the Night")

— Coker's attack on the university group ("Frustration")

— the sudden visitation of the mysterious plague ("Frustration")

— the unexpected appearance of Mr. Torrence ("Strategic Withdrawal")

The second minor device in the narrative is the employment of what might be termed climactic chapter endings. Simply, it means that Wyndham frequently closes a chapter on a critical level which points directly to events in the following chapter, thus holding the reader in suspense for subsequent events. Again, examples make the point clear:

— "Conference" ends with this intriguing statement: "And we danced, on the brink of an unknown future, to an echo from a vanished past." Waiting for that "unknown future" to emerge, the reader, as yet, does not realize that it holds, only hours away, Coker's dramatic assault on the university building.

— "—And Farther On" ends with Brennell's sudden appearance, armed with a rifle, in front of Bill's truck.

— "World Narrowing" closes with the glimpse of Simpson's helicopter, and the restless feeling it arouses in Bill and Josella.

— "Contact," closing with the statement, "But, as things fell out, we were all of us much too busy to try . . .", directly leads to the dramatic happenings of the final chapter, "Strategic Withdrawal."

In summary, a number of conclusions about the structure of *The Day of the Triffids* may be stated:

1. The firm chronology of the events, the concentration on Bill's adventures and the frequent employment of minor narrative devices indicate the importance of the plot element in the novel. It is, first and foremost, an adventure story consisting of dramatic episodes.

2. The Josella sub-plot contributes to the human interest dimension of the novel. Thus, as a character, Josella really helps to develop the plot on only two occasions—when she notices the signal beam from the university tower, and when she mentions

the Sussex farmhouse as a suitable retreat. Apart from those events, her presence is required only for the emotional context which she gives to the book.

3. The Beadley sub-plot contributes to the novel in both a narrative and a philosophical sense. On the one hand, the search for Beadley motivates much of the central portion of the narrative. On the other hand, the Beadley group represents a reaction to catastrophe which is examined and tested in the book.

Style

The primary task facing the writer of science fiction is the creation of a world that is credible to the reader. The task is not easy for, on the one hand, that world has to be sufficiently new and interesting to challenge the imagination and, on the other hand it has to be, in some ways, sufficiently familiar to be credible and acceptable as reality. In *The Day of the Triffids*, the world of the future, as presented by the novelist, has not changed greatly from the world we know. There is, for example, no indication of startling developments in technology that we might regard as strange and unusual. There are, in fact, only two elements in the novel that we might regard as new. The first is the existence in space of a satellite carrying radiation powerful enough to visit upon the whole earth a plague of blindness. The second, obviously related to that, is the development, through mutations of some kind, of a form of plant life with the characteristics of the triffids. However, these two elements are sufficient to create Wyndham's "new" world. The credibility of the ensuing events is achieved by the style of the author which, for the purposes of these Notes, is taken to mean simply the characteristic techniques Wyndham employs in telling his story.

The most obvious characteristic is the use of first person narration. The story is related entirely by Bill Masen. After the catastrophe of May 8, from the security of the Isle of Wight, Bill is recollecting the experiences which befell him after that fateful day. It is his story, seen from his point of view. Wyndham's choice of point of view is important, and contributes important qualities to the narrative:

1. The first-person narration adds to the suspense of the events. Bill re-lives and re-creates the events for us, recapturing his former anxieties and reviving his previous sense of insecurity, so that the catastrophe seems to be happening in the present, and all the threat of lurking danger is felt again. The opening chapter, "The End Begins," is a good example of the suspense which the first-person narration creates. As we share Bill's first feelings of confusion and accompany him on his first stumbling explorations of the hospital, the eerieness and uncertainty of that morning are communicated powerfully.

2. A second achievement of first-person narration is an aspect of the point just discussed. The first person point of view

gives the narrative the authenticity that only a participant can bring. The story is not only an eyewitness account of unusual events; it is the personal story of someone who was involved in those events. Thus, in all that happens—the hand-to-hand combat with triffids, the eerie drives through the ravaged English countryside, the confrontation with Brennell and his menacing rifle, the thrilling escape from Torrence's party—the reader has the sense of being there. The atmosphere of the narrative, then, is not cool and objective; it is personal and, consequently, filled with a sense of involvement.

3. From what has already been said, it is clear that first-person narration also adds to the credibility of the science fiction novel. In a strange world beset by strange disasters, in which the reader's perspective must necessarily be somewhat distorted, the reader needs an anchor in recognizable reality. He must be able to identify in a personal way with some aspect of the story. In *The Day of the Triffids*, Bill Masen is the reader's anchor, because he is a credible human being who experiences credible human emotions. Thus, the reader can understand and identify with Bill's sense of panic during the first waking moments of May 8, with his mood of nostalgia as he looks over the city from the apartment window, with his feelings of sorrow and pity as he leaves the young girl to whom he has given poison, and with his human emotions in almost every situation which he faces. The novel is certainly an adventure story, but it is an adventure story infused with a whole range of credible human emotions. The narrator, Bill Masen, is the source of those responses.

4. Finally, the first-person narration of *The Day of the Triffids* contributes to the pace of the narrative. The fact that the narrator is involved, personally, in most of what happens means that there is no need for awkward changes of scene during which the novelist takes up the threads of various sub-plots, while the main plot involving his hero stands still. Only twice in the novel are present events subordinated to past events. These two occasions are Josella's account of her escape from London and Simpson's account of the adventures of Beadley's group. Thus, events as they actually happen are kept sharply in focus, and the narrative achieves a brisk pace.

A second, important aspect of the style of *The Day of the Triffids* is the distinctive movement of the story with its alternation of action and reflection. Wyndham presents his scenes of action crisply and convincingly. Consider, for example, Bill's struggle with the man attacking Josella:

> I reached the pair as his arm was raised for another stroke. It was easy to snatch the rod from his unexpecting hand and bring it down with some force upon his shoulder. He promptly lashed a heavy boot out in my direction, but I had dodged back quickly, and his radius of action was limited by the cord on his wrists. He made another swiping kick at the air while I was feeling in my pocket for a knife. Finding nothing there, he turned and kicked the girl for good measure, instead. Then he swore at her and pulled on the cord to bring her to her feet. I slapped him on the side of his head, just hard enough to stop him and make his head sing for a bit—somehow I could not bring myself to lay out a blind man, even this type. While he was steadying himself from that I stooped swiftly and cut the cord which joined them. A slight shove on the man's chest sent him staggering back and half turned him so that he lost his bearings. With his freed left hand he let out a final raking swing. It missed me, but ultimately reached the brick wall. After that he lost interest in pretty well everything but the pain of his cracked knuckles. I helped the girl up, loosed her hands, and led her away down the alley while he was still blistering the air behind us.

There are in the novel many other brief episodes which reveal the same crispness and clarity in narrative technique. The following examples might provide a basis for further study:

— the encounter with the triffid at Josella's home
— the tense scene involving Coker's companions in front of the university building
— the attack by the young man with a pistol
— the triffid attack upon Bill's group of blind men
— the finding of Shirning Farm
— the escape from Shirning

However, in addition to describing exciting episodes which are vivid and convincing, Wyndham adds to the texture of the novel in other passages which are noteworthy for their mood magic. Thus, not only is he able to communicate to the reader the physical threats and dangers of a devasted world, he is able, in addition, to create a sense of the human reaction to that world. For example, in "The Groping City," Bill, feeling completely alone and "rudderless," eats his lunch in a garden that had once been the graveyard of a vanished church. The atmosphere, as Wyndham describes it, is heavy with a sense of solitude and desolation. Only an occasional human figure goes shuffling by. One or two sparrows, the first Bill had seen that day, peck indifferently at some crumbs. Then the heavy quietness is broken by the soft notes of a young girl's voice. To the accompaniment of a piano, she is singing a sentimental ballad. As Bill listens, the sadness of the new world floods in upon him:

> I listened, looking up at the pattern that the tender young leaves and the branches made against the fresh blue sky. The song finished. The notes of the piano died away. Then there was a sound of sobbing. No passion: softly, helplessly, forlorn, heartbroken. Who she was, whether it was the singer weeping her hopes away, I do not know. But to listen longer was more than I could endure. I went quietly back into the street, unable to see anything more than mistily for a while.

The moment is brief, and passes quickly. Yet, by means of the fragility of the girl's voice and the brevity of the incident, the heavy weight of the sadness of the world is felt sharply and memorably. Wyndham is also able to create mood by using a larger canvas. For example, later, in "A Light in the Night," Bill looks out from the apartment window upon the silent city of London. The sun is sinking in the sky, and black smudges of smoke dot the landscape. As he watches reflectively, he has a strong sense of the disappearance of a world which is succumbing to "the long, slow, inevitable course of decay and collapse." The truth, horrifying and inevitable, comes to him forcefully, in spite of the vague optimism that seems to be characteristic of all human beings:

It must be, I thought, one of the race's most persistent and comforting hallucinations to trust that "it can't happen here"—that one's own little time and place is beyond cataclysms. And now it was happening here. Unless there should be some miracle, I was looking on the beginning of the end of London—and very likely, it seemed, there were other men, not unlike me, who were looking at the beginning of the end of New York, Paris, San Francisco, Buenos Aires, Bombay, and all the rest of the cities that were destined to go the way of those others under the jungles.

Here, the size of the canvas and the sense of nostalgia created by the roll call of the great cities of the world contribute to the heavy mood of inevitable doom.

Clearly, then, some of the effectiveness of the narrative finds its source in Wyndham's technique of narration. The novel is basically episodic—as has been said before, it is, at heart, an adventure story—but the human response is not ignored. There are, thus, many passages in which human emotions—nostalgia, despair, sorrow, determination—illuminate the story and give it that texture that lends credibility.

Purpose and Theme

Ray Bradbury, the American author of such well-known science fiction works as *Fahrenheit 451* and *The Martian Chronicles*, has frequently emphasized the social purpose of his writing. His task, as he has made clear, is not simply that of entertainment:

> I think that science-fiction and fantasy offer the liveliest, freshest approaches to many of our problems today, and I always hope to write in this vivid and vigorous form, saying what I think about philosophy and sociology in our immediate future. An ancestor of mine, Mary Bradbury, was tried as a witch in Salem in the seventeenth-century; from her, I suppose, I get my concern and dedicated interest in freedom from fear and a detestation for thought-investigation or thought-control of any sort. Science-fiction is a wonderful hammer; I intend to use it when and if necessary, to bark a few shins or knock a few heads, in order to make people leave people alone.

There can be few clearer statements by a writer of his purpose in writing. Bradbury's purpose in his writing is obviously to elevate the human principle in life. Faced with a world that daily grows more complex, that is more and more dominated by technology, Bradbury sees the real danger as being the loss of the human element and, in his writing, emphasizes the cruciality of spiritual and cultural concerns.

The same kind of concern has illuminated the writing of John Wyndham. This can be demonstrated by examining *The Chrysalids*, another of his widely read science fiction novels. In *The Chrysalids*, Wyndham turns once more to the world of the future. It is a world of miserable misfortune. Some kind of atomic holocaust has destroyed civilization, so that all that remain are isolated pockets of human population. Further, the life which remains is plagued by the effects of radiation, which plays strange tricks upon all forms of life. Thus, plants, animals and human forms of life often appear with strange characteristics. Faced with these bewildering variations, Waknuk, the community in the novel, tries to achieve a sense of order in the midst of the obvious disorder. The people base their religion on the sanctity of the old forms of life. Man, they declare, was made in the image of God; therefore, any variation from that accepted image is a curse. Consequently, their society engages in a ruthless destruction of all forms of life which are thought to deviate from the accepted norms. Deviant plants are burned; deviant animals are slaughtered; and deviant humans are either banished or executed. As a result, the life of the community is marked by fear and sorrow. Moreover, with such a rigid view of what is normal and acceptable, the community becomes static. Change is impossible in view of the bigoted, narrow nature of the minds of the people. There is, then, Wyndham seems to be saying, no future for such a race of people. Chained to the past, they cannot adapt to the present dynamically, and they are unable to conceive of the future in any different terms. Their doom is inevitable, as the representative of the New People of Sealand explained:

> The unhappy Fringes people were condemned through no act of their own to a life of squalor and misery—there could be no future for them. As for those who condemned them—well, that, too, is the way of it. There have been lords of life before, you know. Did you ever hear of the great lizards? When the time came for them to be superseded they had to pass away.

However, it is important to note that Wyndham is not simply condemning the attitudes of the Waknuk people. Through them, he is judging the people of the twentieth century. The Waknuk people failed because their attitudes were inherited from those of the world before the holocaust. The Old People—the people of the twentieth century—were also at fault:

> . . .They were only ingenious half-humans, little better than savages; all living shut off from one another, with only clumsy words to link them. Often they were shut off still more by different languages, and different beliefs. Some of them could think individually, but they had to remain individuals. Emotions they could sometimes share, but they could not think collectively.

When their conditions were primitive they could get along all right, as the animals can; but the more complex they made their world, the less capable they were of dealing with it. They had no means of consensus. They learned to co-operate constructively in small units; but only destructively in large untis. They aspired greedily, and then refused to face the responsibilities they had created. They created vast problems, and then buried their heads in the sands of idle faith. There was, you see, no real communication, no understanding between them. They could, at their best, be near-sublime animals, but not more.

They could never have succeeded. If they had not brought down Tribulation which all but destroyed them; then they would have bred with the carelessness of animals until they had reduced themselves to poverty and misery, and ultimately to starvation and barbarism. One way or another they were foredoomed because they were an inadequate species.

This indictment of the human race is startling and compelling. It is an indictment of men and women today, and of the world which they have created. The charges against contemporary humanity are clear:

1. People have isolated themselves from one another. Languages, beliefs and nationality have split the human race, so that meaningful communication has been inhibited.

2. The complexity of the world constructed by twentieth-century man demands co-operation upon the widest scale, but he has shown himself unequal to the demands.

3. In creating a complex society, man was faced with new responsibilities which he refused to assume. One such responsibility would be, for example, the difficulties caused by an expanding population.

4. The key to twentieth-century man's activity was his greed.

5. Confronted with vast problems, twentieth-century man ignored the dangers and difficulties he had created.

Thus, *The Chrysalids* is an impressive, moving analysis of the problems of modern man. In a sense, the novel is a declaration that the central problem is man himself. Man, it supremacy in the universe, clinging to the folly of national barriers and ignoring the threats to existence created by himself, is slowly destroying all that he cherishes and all that is best in his race.

In its own way, *The Day of the Triffids* expresses a strong point of view about modern man and his existence. At first, the world Bill Masen knew before May 8, the day he awoke to a blinded society, was idyllic. Many of the problems that plague us today had been solved and, for most people, existence was characterized by peace and plenty, as Bill himself explains:

> The world we lived in was wide, and most of it was open to us with little trouble. Roads, railways, and shipping lines laced it, ready to carry one thousands of miles safely and in comfort. If we wanted to travel more swiftly still, and could afford it, we traveled by airplane. There was no need for anyone to take weapons or even precautions in those days. You could go just as you were to wherever you wished, with nothing to hinder you—other than a lot of forms and regulations.

With such stability, there came material progress, which aimed at feeding the world's population:

> It must be difficult for young people who never knew it to envisage a world like that. Perhaps it sounds like a golden age—though it wasn't quite that to those who lived in it. Or they may think that an Earth ordered and cultivated almost all over sounds dull—but it wasn't that either. It was rather an exciting place—for a biologist anyway. Every year we were pushing the northern limit of growth for food plants a little further back. New fields were growing quick crops on what had historically been simply tundra or barren land. Every season, too, stretches of desert both old and recent were reclaimed and made to grow grass or food. For food was then our most pressing problem, and the progress of the regeneration schemes, and the advance of the cultivation lines on the maps, was followed with

almost as much attention as an earlier generation had paid to battle fronts.

Reading this account, one naturally wonders what could have gone wrong in such a world. If food preoccupied the energies of man more than did war, how could the future not have been assured? Bill was able to identify the cause for the misfortune that came. In the old situation, many had interpreted their period of peace as a sign of change in the nature of man. The turning from swords to plowshares was claimed as evidence of a new human spirit abroad in the world. Bill came to know better, for—in spite of appearances—the world, and especially the people in it, continued much as before: 95 per cent of the people wanted to live in peace, but a persistent 5 per cent still thought of war, and of the benefits to be gained by war. That was one important negative factor in the situation. The second factor was human greed. Thus, huge companies, when they were deprived of their monopolies in products, began to engage in competition. For this reason, the Arctic & European Fish Oil Company was attracted by the sample of triffid oil brought to them by Umberto Christoforo Palanguez. They saw immediately that his oil was far superior to their best fish oils, and paid Umberto an enormous sum of money to fly out triffid seeds from Russia. That mission, according to Bill's conjecture, led to the disastrous proliferation of triffids over the earth, since Umberto's plane was probably downed by the Russians. It is clear, then, that in Bill's view the catastrophe which visited earth on May 8 sprang from two causes. The first was the warring element in human society; the second was the dangerous, widespread presence of the triffids. Bill was confident of his analysis of what had happened. No comet, he insisted, had been responsible for the blindness that had afflicted men everywhere. The affliction had come, he explained to Josella, from loaded satellites which suspicious, warring nations had circling the earth:

"Up there," I went on, "up there there were—and maybe there still are—unknown numbers of satellite weapons circling round and round the Earth. Just a lot of dormant menaces, touring around, waiting for someone, or something, to set them off. What was in

145

them? You don't know; I don't know. Top-secret stuff. All we've heard is guesses—fissile materials, radioactive dusts, bacteria, viruses. . . . Now suppose that one type happened to have been constructed especially to emit radiations that our eyes would not stand—something that would burn out or at least damage the optic nerve."

The conclusion was plain: "somehow or other we brought this lot down on ourselves." The catastrophe could be laid at the door of man's suspicion of his fellow man, of the warring spirit that man finds it so hard to quell, of man's inability to live in peace and tranquillity. Moreover, the tragedy was compounded by another unfortunate aspect of man's nature: his greedy pursuit of profitable discoveries. The major fault here is not so much man's greed, perhaps, as man's irresponsible passion to discover and invent. In our own world of today, one of the urgent problems facing our society is the need to develp moral concepts to deal acceptably with the technological world we have created. For example, the invention of the hydrogen bomb has brought to the world moral problems which are still unresolved. Man's technology is frequently sophisticated; his moral nature is frequently unsophisticated. The same problem plagued the world as Bill had known it. Thus, though no one could be blamed directly for the ravaging triffids, nonetheless man's insatiable urge to discover contributed to the tragedy:

> I don't think we can blame anyone too much for the triffids. The extracts they gave were very valuable in the circumstances. Nobody can ever see what a major discovery is going to lead to—whether it is a new kind of engine or a triffid—and we coped with them all right in normal conditions. We benefited quite a lot from them, as long as the conditions were to their disadvantage.

Here, Bill's claims for the innocence of man sound somewhat shrill. Whatever the explanation for the devastation wrought by the triffids, the hands of man were not clean, and it is clear that, in some sense, he had brought this tragedy, too, upon himself.

This rather lengthy discussion makes one point abundantly clear: that John Wyndham's novel is not purely an adventure story, intended to divert and entertain its readers. At the heart of the novel, there are shrewd observations about human nature and human existence. An examination of *The Day of the Triffids* makes a number of these observations clear. They may be summarized as follows:

1. The novel emphasizes the persistent inability of man to live at peace with his fellows. Before May 8, the world of Bill Masen had been one of steady material progress. Man had devoted most of his energies to providing food for the world's population. Deserts had been made fruitful, and arid wastes had been forced to yield harvests. Devoted to the conquest of hunger and want, men had lived in peace. And yet, in spite of the wishes of the majority, it had been an uneasy peace. The warring spirit had remained. Its symbols were the satellites circling the globe, loaded with deadly materials. Like so many time bombs, they had hovered over the earth until, by accident or by design, their deadly contents had blanketed the world. Thus, man's suspicion of man had wrought its work, and people everywhere awoke to darkness. The lesson for our own world is as obvious as it is uncomfortable, for we live in an era that is constantly corrupted by the poison of war, whether it appears in Korea, Viet Nam or the Middle East.

2. In the second place, the novel suggests the need for man to develop a moral sensitivity in keeping with his technological sophistication. However complex the world may become, man must recognize his responsibility for it. Josella understands that, in a way, that responsibility is a welcome burden, for it is man's assurance that he lives in a rational universe, as she explains in responding to Bill's account of the tragedy that had visited the world:

> I suppose, in a way, that should be more horrible than the idea of nature striking blindly at us. And yet I don't think it is. It makes me feel less hopeless about things because it makes them at least comprehensible. If it *was* like that, then it is at least a thing that can be prevented from happening again—just one more of the mistakes our very great grand-children are going to have to avoid. And, oh dear, there were so many, many mistakes! But we can warn them.

The message is abundantly plain. Man cannot live on this planet in complete indifference. Each step forward that he makes is accompanied by the possibility of error. It is, then, his duty to consider his way with care and to avoid the mistakes of the past. Man cannot live arrogantly; he must live thoughtfully.

3. To live with awareness of the dangers within himself and the dangers he creates in his own world, man must be conscious of his own fragile position in the universe. Traditionally, man has sought to stress his permanence in the universe. Though his life is brief, he has laid claim to immortality through his accomplishments. His artistic creations, his technological advances, the durability of his institutions and the multiplication of his species have given him a confidence in the world that he is, perhaps, not justified in possessing. Believing himself to be made just a little lower than the angels and to be granted dominion over all things, he has often assumed himself to be lord of the universe. Wyndham shows us clearly in *The Day of the Triffids* the danger of such an arrogant assumption. Walter Lucknor understood the real situation. From his study of the triffids he had learned that man's superiority depended upon characteristics that men take for granted, but that are, nonetheless, vital for his very survival. The triffids, he saw,

> . . . know what is the surest way to put a man out of action—in other words, they know what they're doing. Look at it this way. Granted that they do have intelligence; then that would leave us with only one important superiority—sight. We can see, and they can't. Take away our vision, and the superiority is gone. Worse than that—our position becomes inferior to theirs, because they are adapted to a sightless existence and we are not.

In such a situation, sight, a capability accepted without thought by man, is a crucial gift. Faced with creatures that also possess an intelligence and that can communicate with one another, man's sole asset, the single basis for his superiority, is his vision. Robbed of that, man loses all claim to his superiority. Being human, then, has no particular meaning, for man's very survival is shrouded in uncertainty. Lucknor perceived the real danger of the new situation:

. . . what's the good of our ability to handle things if we can't see what to do with them? Anyway, they don't need to handle things—not in the way we do. They can get their nourishment direct from the soil, or from insects and bits of raw meat. They don't have to go through all the complicated business of growing things, distributing them, and usually cooking them as well. In fact, if it were a choice for survival between a triffid and a blind man, I know which I'd put my money on.

The point here is not whether such a startling situation could come to pass. In fact, in choosing plants as the threat to the existence of man, Wyndham seems to be stretching, probably deliberately, our credulity to its utmost. The choice is intended to startle, and to make us aware of the truth embodied in the threat: that we need to consider more carefully and more sensitively our position in the universe. For it would seem that the warning is given that that position is not one of guaranteed supremacy. Man is simply one aspect of creation, and if his race is to continue, then he must exercise his powers with responsibility and accept his role with humility.

4. If man is a fragile creature in the universe, it follows that his institutions are similarly fragile. Nevertheless, man thinks and acts as though his social order were permanent. Just as he thinks of himself as permanent, so he accepts social organization as permanent. It is as though that organization were an unalterable factor in the universe. In fact, such human confidence is an illusion, as Wyndham makes clear. For example, at first Bill Masen's training and experience render him incapable of accepting the reality of the tragedy that has afflicted mankind. Initially, he clings to the illusion of permanence, and expects the old world to be restored suddenly:

Nevertheless, it was hard to persuade oneself to do that smash a window. I was not yet ready to admit, after nearly thirty years of a reasonably right-respecting existence and law-abiding life, that things had changed in any fundamental was. There was, too, a feeling that as long as I remained *my* normal self things might even yet, in some inconceivable way, return to *their* normal. Absurd it undoubtedly was, but I had a very strong sense that the moment I should stove in one of those sheets of plate glass I would leave the old order behind me forever: I should become a looter, a sacker, a low scavenger upon the dead body of the system that had nourished me.

However, Bill's hesitation soon passes, as he is forced to recognize the disappearance of civilized institutions and behavior. All around him, he perceived that people were "already fast losing ordinary restraints." Witnessing struggling mobs competing for merchandise from the stores, he saw plainly that:

> What was going on was a grim business without chivalry, with no give, and all take, about it. A man bumping into another and feeling that he carried a parcel would snatch it and duck away, on the chance that it contained something to eat, while the loser clutched furiously at the air or hit out indiscriminately. Once I had to step hurriedly aside to avoid being knocked down by an elderly man who darted into the roadway with no care for possible obstacles. His expression was vastly cunning, and he clutched avariciously to his chest two cans of red paint. On a corner my way was blocked by a group almost weeping with frustration over a bewildered child who could see but was just too young to understand what they wanted of it.

Not only has the stability of civilized law and order been swept away; other features of civilization crumble also. Thus, in "Frustration," the young girl who approaches Bill with the offer of her companionship is the innocent victim of a vanishing moral order, for she offers herself to him in order to persuade him to stay with the group of blind men. Similarly, religion is seen to be shattered as a force in civilization. Miss Durrant's group is an attempt to save the race by establishing a remnant which will live according to Christian principles. The attempt is doomed almost at the outset. The vicar, who is the spiritual leader of the party, is full of good intentions, but his impractical religious concepts are seen as leading inevitably to failure. As

Coker observes, if the vicar's prayer for more blind people to join the group were granted, "the whole place would become entirely unworkable." In contrast, it is worth noting, Beadley's party is organized, not according to traditional Christian precepts, but according to the new social teachings of Dr. Vorless. The entire picture is, then, one of the crumbling of trusted institutions and beliefs, which man accepts, unthinkingly, as permanent. The truth is that man's institutions and customs are as fragile as man himself.

5. A natural result of his last point is Wyndham's seemingly humanistic view of existence. Religion is not presented as a vital, or even viable, force in the novel. There is no sense of a Christian God watching over the affairs of men and caring compassionately for his creatures. The world of the novel is a world without God. Thus, if man is to be saved—that is, if he is to survive—then he must do so by his own efforts. No mystical power will aid him, for the universe Wyndham presents is primarily a rational universe, in which survival is achieved by the exercise of one's will and intelligence. This truth is the burden of Josella's words, when she replies to Bill's explanation of the causes of the tragedy that had befallen the world:

> "I suppose, in a way, that should be more horrible than the idea of nature striking blindly at us. And yet I don't think it is. It makes me feel less hopeless about things because it makes them at least comprehensible. If it *was* like that, then it is at least a thing that can be prevented from happening again— just one more of the mistakes our very great grandchildren are going to have to avoid."

As she speaks, it is obvious that she does not see in what has happened any sense of a divine judgment; nor does she look for any divine intervention. What happened was caused by "mistakes." In the future, man must avoid such errors. Exercising care, he will, by intelligence, save the future for himself. In fact, this is the novel's final picture of the universe, as Bill looks to the future:

> So we must think of the task ahead as ours alone.
> We believe now that we can see our way, but there is

still a lot of work and research to be done before the day when we, or our children, or their children, will cross the narrow straits on a great crusade to drive the triffids back and back with ceaseless destruction until we have wiped out the last one of them from the face of the land that they have usurped.

The talk of a crusade is a religious expression, but it is the religion of man, and not the religion of God.

6. Finally, *The Day of the Triffids* presents an optimistic view of man. It is true that the ugliness of man's nature is often laid bare in the novel. Many unfortunate aspects of man—his indifference to others, his gross selfishness, his utter cruelty, his bigotry—are clearly portrayed. In this regard, the following scenes provide more than adequate testimony to man's inhumanity:

—the line of blind men at Piccadilly Circus
—the looters in Soho
—the man who captured Josella
—the crowd who stopped Bill's car
—the strife in front of the university building
—the young man with the pistol
—the people in Brighton

And yet, the novel says much of a different kind. On many occasions, Wyndham also shows us a different aspect of human beings. Human beings are often portrayed as creatures capable of tender, attractive feelings. For example, the novel does stress the inherent pathos of human life. People, no matter how harshly we may judge them, are viewed as doing the best they can in adverse circumstances and are, thus, not to be criticized severely. Since the human condition is essentially tragic, then, human beings are to be pitied rather than condemned. An example of this attitude is provided by the girl whom Bill hears singing. At such a moment, there is no bitter denunciation of the human folly that has caused catastrophe; there is only compassionate feeling for the sorrow that the hour has brought. Similarly, Bill's recollection of the young girl who offered herself to him on behalf of the blind men is movingly tender. She had shown Bill the kind of self-sacrifice of which human beings are capable, for she had not asked him to take her with him—she had asked him to stay with the blind men. She is, thus, an illustration of man's capacity for elevating and expressing the things of the spirit, rather than practical and material considerations. This same spiritual resilience is displayed by Miss Durrant's party. It is true that their efforts are doomed; it is true that their neglect of practical considerations renders their endeavors hopeless. Yet, in a sense they are admirable for, in the face of staggering adversity, they cling to their religious principles. In even larger measure, the little group at Shirning Farm evokes similar admiration. Isolated and outnumbered, they live and love in the face of incredible odds. Their struggle is eloquent testimony to all that is best in human nature. Consequently, it is clear that *The Day of the Triffids* is not entirely an indictment of the human race. In portraying their dogged persistence, their quiet fortitude, their resilient courage, their ingenious inventiveness, their tender love and their sensitive feelings, the novel leaves us with a sense of the admirable complexity that is man.

Such are some of the implications of the novel. Careful consideration of these ideas would seem to lead us to conclude that John Wyndham is seeking to make a serious statement in the novel about human beings and their existence. His theme would seem to be that contemporary man, blinded by his arrogant egotism and plagued by his inability to work with his fellows, needs to awaken to all that is best within himself. Thus, by drawing upon the profound resources of his intelligence and the deepest treasures of his compassion, he may yet build a world whose beauty, variety and richness he truly appreciates.

Suggested Study Topics

1. Ray Bradbury, the author of *Fahrenheit 451*, described science fiction as "a wonderful hammer." What evidence do you find in *The Day of the Triffids* to suggest what Wyndham was similarly interested in offering social criticism to his contemporaries?

2. Is *The Day of the Triffids* simply an exciting adventure story? Discuss the answer to this question, using an analysis of the plot structure to support your thesis.

3. Give an account of the triffids, explaining:
   a. their characteristics
   b. the nature of the threat they posed to man
   c. the possibilities of their eventual control.

4. Give an account of the character of Bill Masen, suggesting reasons for his suitability as the hero of the novel.

5. Describe any three minor characters, and explain the nature of their contribution to the plot.

6. Wyndham's novels have been described as being weak in characterization. Show the truth of this statement by analyzing three or four of the characters in *The Day of the Triffids*.

7. Present what you regard as a major theme in the novel. Justify your choice with specific references to the novel.

8. Discuss the methods used by John Wyndham to create an air of credibility in *The Day of the Triffids*.

Bibliography

Wyndham's Works

As John Beynon
The Secret People, 1935.
Foul Play Suspected, 1935.
The Planet Plane, 1936.

As John Wyndham
The Day of the Triffids, 1951.
The Kraken Wakes, 1953.
Jizzle, and Other Stories, 1954.
The Chrysalids, 1955.
The Seeds of Time, 1956.
Tales of Gooseflesh and Laughter, 1956.
The Midwich Cuckoos, 1957.
The Outward Urge, 1959.
Trouble and Lichen, 1960.
Consider Her Ways, 1961.
The Infinite Moment, 1961.
The John Wyndham Omnibus, 1964.
Chocky, 1968.

Criticisms
Aldiss, Brian W. *Billion Year Spree: The True History of Science Fiction*. Garden City, N.Y.: Doubleday, 1973.
Atheling, Jr. William. (James Blish) *The Issue at Hand*. Chicago: Advent, 1964.
_____. *More Issues at Hand*. Chicago: Advent, 1972.
Bretnor, Reginald, ed. *Modern Science Fiction: Its Meaning and Its Future*. New York: Coward-McCann, 1953.
_____. *Science Fiction, Today and Tomorrow*. New York: Harper and Row, 1974.
Clareson, Thomas D., ed. *SF: The Other Side of Realism*. Bowling Green, Ohio: Bowling Green University Popular Press, 1971.
_____. *Science Fiction Criticism: An Annotated Checklist*. Kent, Ohio: Kent State University Press, 1972.
Franklin, H. Bruce. *Future Perfect: American Science Fiction of the Nineteenth Century*. New York: Oxford University Press, 1966.

Gunn, James. *Alternate Worlds: The Illustrated History of Science Fiction.* Englewood Cliffs, N.J.: Prentice-Hall, Inc., 1975.

Hillegas, Mark R. *The Future as Nightmare: H.G. Wells and the Anti-Utopians.* New York: Oxford University Press, 1967.

Knight, Damon. *In Search of Wonder.* Chicago: Advent, 1967.

Moskowitz, Sam. *Explorers of the Infinite: Shapers of Science Fiction.* Cleveland: World, 1963.

_____. *Seekers of Tomorrow: Masters of Modern Science Fiction.* Cleveland, 1966.

Scholes, Robert. *Structural Fabulation: An Essay on Fiction of the Future.* Notre Dame: University of Notre Dame Press, 1975.